You both also lead inspiring lives! With love from us all,

Nelle.

Much, much love on your anniversary!

Marion & John

November 25, 1995

TOUCH OF
THE SHEPHERD

Also by Celestine Sibley

A Place Called Sweet Apple
Ah, Sweet Mystery
Children, My Children
Christmas in Georgia
Day By Day
Dear Store
Dire Happenings in Scratch Ankle
Especially at Christmas
For All Seasons
Jincey
The Magic Realm of Sallie Middleton
The Malignant Heart
Mothers Are Always Special
Peachtree Street, U.S.A.
Small Blessings
The Sweet Apple Gardening Book
Tokens of Myself
Turned Funny
Young 'uns

Work In Progress

A Plague of Kinfolks

TOUCH OF THE SHEPHERD

Reflections on the Life
of Vernon S. Broyles, Jr.

By Celestine Sibley

Editor
Sandra J. Still, Ph.D.

Layout & Design
Penstroke Graphics
Atlanta, Georgia

Project Consultant
R. Bemis Publishing, Ltd.
Marietta, Georgia 30007

Back Cover Photograph
Gittings
Atlanta, Georgia

Library of Congress Catalogue: CIP

ISBN: 0-89176-043-1

First printing: March, 1994

Proceeds from the sale of TOUCH OF THE SHEPHERD: Reflections on the Life of Vernon S. Broyles, Jr., will be donated to the BROYLES MINISTRY CENTER of the North Avenue Presbyterian Church, U.S.A.

FOREWORD

Walk worthy of the vocation wherewith ye are called.

Eph. 4:1

He had not been my minister for a number of years. He retired from North Avenue Presbyterian Church and I transferred my membership to a smaller Roswell Presbyterian church near the little log cabin in the country to which I had moved. But we stayed in touch. He called occasionally and after I married the second time I took my husband up to the mountains of North Georgia to get acquainted with him and to hear him preach in the beautiful chapel he had inspired and helped to build. We had dinner on its sunny deck with him and his second wife and members of that church.

He had seen me though troubles and grief, offering comfort, sometimes direction and often heartening laughter. His friendship meant a great deal to me. So when he called me one morning in the spring of 1991 and asked me if I would do a favor for him, "Sure," I answered without hesitation. "Tell me what."

He explained. A group of Atlanta men, who had been powerful forces in all his accomplishments in church, school, and charitable undertakings, and were also close friends, had decided that his life was a story that should be told. He didn't agree but they persisted. He was eighty-seven years old. They wanted a book written about him.

"I'm tired of trying to change their minds," he said. "I don't want to write about myself. I don't see anything that needs to be written. But they are persisting and finally I told them that the only way I would sit still for a book would be if you wrote it."

"Do you want me to say 'no'?" I asked, thinking he might be using me as a means of avoiding the whole project. Would it get him off the hook if I declined?

"No,", he said. "They are determined."

"Okay, I'll do it," I said. And added belatedly, "I'm honored that you'd ask me."

His old deep, joyous chortle, a mixture of dismay and pleasure in the ridiculous, vibrated in the telephone.

"No hurry," he said. "Take your time—but I am eighty-seven years old."

I couldn't hurry. I had other commitments — a daily job at the newspaper, a book to finish, a projected trip to Italy to visit my New York editor with my daughter. It would be October before I could get started. And when I did begin to think about it, I was discouraged.

"You know," I told him when we sat in his mountain study one day, "The story of a good man, leading a good life, ain't necessarily a good book. It'd be a lot easier for me to do a book on Jimmy Swaggart."

He laughingly agreed.

"I know," he said. "The good-man-good-life thing is not the reality you think it is anyhow." He hesitated, not wanting to make a comparison with his scandalous brother in the ministry, Mr. Swaggart. "You want to call this deal off?"

Suddenly I didn't. The more I learned about the details of his eighty-seven years, the more it seemed to me that a good man leading a good life may be the best story of all.

His faith was often awesome to me. I found myself wondering if such a bulwark could be possible in my own life. (Is there enough of this to go around? I asked in effect.) He had a curious hunger to know the will of God. Curious, that is, to laissez-faire Christians who incline to the what-you-don't-know-won't-hurt-you theory. He was, he'd be the first to say, an ordinary man, but he made an extraordinary impact on his region and in the religious world of all denominations and on scores of troubled, seeking individuals.

So I took on the assignment, working at it when other concerns permitted, talking to scores of people he had helped or who had helped him, and reading his sermons and portions of his diary. Every new fact brought up a new question, and we talked often over the phone, meeting for lunch when we could. By early February I had asked to see his mother's letters, more of his diary, a battered old scrapbook he kept as a child, and an assortment of the columns he had written for our newspaper back in the fifties.

We made an appointment. I was to drive up to his house in the mountain resort, Big Canoe, in mid-afternoon. He had told me a few days before that he was retiring—again—and that the coming Sunday would be one of his last sermons.

"What will you do?" I asked, appalled to think that his life — jammed with the urgent, pressing concerns of God and man — might suddenly be empty.

He laughed.

"Between the time I preach my last sermon and the time I die, I may have a great adventure," he said.

Big Canoe is a beautiful resort development, launched years ago by Dr. Broyles's friend, Tom Cousins. Mr. Cousins had given him the lot on which his retirement house stood, and several other friends and members of North Avenue church joined in to build for him and his wife the gray clapboard and stone cottage on a ridge overlooking a valley and mountains beyond. I always had trouble finding it because of the cunning way the roads into the forest had been laid out, curving around mountains, dipping into valleys, skirting lakes and golf course, and crossing little rustic bridges over rushing streams. The "village" in which the chapel was situated was the only spot where buildings stood out. Most houses were well hidden in woods behind rocky banks of laurel and rhododendron. As a result, Dr. Broyles always asked visitors to call from the gate house, where a security guard was on duty, and he would then meet them a mile or so into the resort at a cross-road.

I called, apologetic because I was running late.

To my surprise the guard spoke into the phone and turned back to ask, "Is he expecting you?" And then, "What did you say your name is?"

Only when his wife, Eloise, met me at the crossroad did I realize Dr. Broyles had forgotten our appointment and wasn't certain of my identity.

He was asleep, Eloise said, and seemed foggy about the whole appointment when the phone awakened him. But when we got to the house he was dressed and waiting for me. He looked pale and tired, but he said the nap had done him good, and he led the way into his study. I handed him the list of names of people I had talked to and asked if he wanted to add any. He glanced at it and put it on his desk, making a joke about the fact that some of his friends were "very imaginative."

We chatted a minute, and suddenly it seemed to me that he was caving in with weariness, his handsome old face as gray as his hair.

I stood up and reached for the material he had put on a table for me. He said I should stay and ask my questions. He felt well enough for that. But I made an excuse about getting out of the mountains before dark, and he followed me to the door. I shook his hand and said, "Go back to bed," and he said gravely, "I think I will."

Eloise led me back to the crossroad, and I got out of my car and walked over to hers to thank her. I lingered moments, wondering if it was presumptuous for me to tell her how ill I thought he was, how urgent his condition might be.

All the way back to Atlanta I worried about him, wondering if there had been anything I could have done. The Broyleses did it themselves. A few hours later they called a doctor, who sent an ambulance, and early the next morning Dr. Broyles was wheeled into Crawford Long Hospital's operating room for open-heart surgery. By the time I got there his three children, grandchildren, and countless friends had come to wait out the operation.

One of the first to arrive was Dr. James Long, the current pastor of North Avenue Presbyterian Church. He came as he was when they called him—and stayed all day. Several times during the long vigil one of the team of physicians would leave the operating room and come with a report. The information was always discouraging. Dr. Broyles was not expected to live. At these times the group in the room, including the doctor and the minister, would clasp hands and bow their heads in prayer.

Toward the end of the day I mentioned to the young minister that he seemed to be praying more for those of us who waited than for Dr. Broyles.

He nodded. Dr. Broyles, he said, was like a very old Scotsman who was near death. His grandson came to read the Bible to him and asked, "Grandpa, what do you want to hear?"

The old man shook his head. "Nothing, lad. My roof is already thatched."

Vernon Broyles, with a lifetime of service to the church and to the community, had thatched his roof.

He died the next morning without regaining consciousness. His children had a private family service at a graveside in West View Cemetery the day following, and after that Atlantans of all denominations and all ages poured into North Avenue sanctuary for a memorial service.

It was a magnificent leave-taking, arrangements for which were literally taken out of the family's hands by the community that loved him. The big church choir was joined by the famous singers from Westminster Schools, which he helped to found and headed for twenty-five years. The organ was supplemented by trombones, trumpets, and tympani from the Atlanta Symphony. His favorite "Battle Hymn of Republic" triumphantly filled the old church with a glorious paean to "the coming of the Lord." The congregation was invited to join in singing the last chorus, but some of us stumbled to our feet blinded by tears. The choir and the young Westminster singers took over for the final verse. Dr. Long and the Reverend Cook Freeman, who had served with Dr. Broyles as associate pastor for twenty-five years, spoke simply and briefly. Dr. Broyles's son, Cap, the Reverend Vernon Broyles III, expressed the family's gratitude for the sympathy and affection that their father's beloved town had shown him.

Finally, suddenly and unexpectedly, the singers and the organ, the trumpets and trombones swept triumphantly into Handel's "Hallelujah Chorus."

Those who had cried smiled and hugged one another and went to his wife and children. Some of us remembered his prayer at the time of the death of a beloved. "Grant that we shall not forsake Thee but going forth from this place shall live more generously, more kindly, more lovingly."

From the old downtown church his family and many of his friends drove to the little mountain chapel he had inspired and helped to build sixty miles away at Appalachia's beginning in the misty hills of Big Canoe, Georgia.

A throng of Big Canoe residents and mountain people met them there. His grandson, Allen, played "Amazing Grace" on the piano. The Reverend Albert Harris, co-pastor of the chapel, spoke of his joyousness, his literal obedience to the Biblical admonition to "rejoice in the Lord" and to "have no anxiety; if you pray and thank him, God will work out the knottiest of our problems."

The Reverend Wayne Smith, a long-time associate and close friend, who had flown home from Russia to be there, spoke of the "shepherd's prayer," the Twenty-third Psalm, and compared Dr. Broyles to the biblical shepherds, who stood by the fold and greeted their sheep as they came in at the end of the day. Like them, he anointed with the oil of kindness the heads of those with wounds from the day's encounter with life's brambles. He touched them and knew each of them.

"Vernon Broyles," said Mr. Smith, "had the touch of the shepherd."

The congregation sang a hymn and said a prayer and stood outside talking of him. There were laughter and a few tears and a sense of rightness that he had done as he wished and moved on to another place.

Perhaps his "great adventure" had just begun.

Love is necessary. Unless you have love in your hearts it does not make much differ-ence what you do. Anything you do will be a failure. No matter how smart you are or how gifted or how much you accomplish as the world counts it, you are wasting your life if you do not have love.
                    VSB sermon

The young Atlanta salesman was experi-encing the usual aridness of Sunday morn-ing. Churches were about the only establish-ments open and operating. He regarded him-self as a non-believer, but he was searching for an allegiance to something higher than himself. He liked music and a good speech and often dropped into a church to see what he might find.

He had visited several Atlanta churches over a period of weeks, and one morning he happened to drop into the old, gray granite pile on the corner of Peachtree Street and North Avenue.

The quartet of professional singers performed well and the sermon held his attention. If not particularly inspired, he was withal content. Then the minister said a prayer—the kind of summing up on most church programs. The young man found himself listening in something akin to awe.

"That man," he said later, "believed he was talking to God! He really believed there was somebody up there!"

The next Sunday he went back and it happened again. The prayer clerics sometimes call "horizontal," aimed at the congregation, was vertical, directed upward.

Again the young man studied the minister curiously. Was he some kind of nut? Or was he a saint?

"He was sincere!" the young man said. "He believed he was talking to God!"

It was a phenomenon to the young man, and he thought about it often during the weeks he was trying to sell pre-fabricated houses to aspiring homeowners. Odd and unsettling as it was, however, he had a personal problem more urgent and insistent.

There was a girl, a pretty school teacher, and he believed he loved her. He felt that she loved him, but he wasn't sure he was ready for marriage. He had led her to believe that he was. He even had a ring to give her. But still...

He thought of the minister who talked to God. Maybe he had an answer. He went back to the church on the downtown corner. The minister received him in his study and heard him out. He gave the best advice he could for one not specializing in problems of the love-lorn. It was better to know before the fact, if you were uncertain about marriage. It was well to wait and think and perhaps to pray over it. They talked enough for the young man to feel some sense of resolve, and he arose to go. At the door he turned.

"How do you get faith?" he asked.

This was the minister's field. He told him three definite things to do: Pray. Read the Bible daily. Go to church—some church, any church—once a week.

"You may receive the gift of faith," he said. "You may not. But it's worth a try." And then he said a prayer.

That night the young man went to see his girl and confessed to her that he had second thoughts about marriage. Hurt but bolstered by a sturdy pride, she took the decision coolly with her head up. But she did want to know whom her no-longer-fiance had been talking to.

A minister, he admitted, one he scarcely knew at an old Presbyterian church on a downtown street corner.

The girl, a staunch Episcopalian, thought scornfully that it might be some kind of Presbyterian meddling and that she didn't care anyhow. But during the week she found she did care. She was in the midst of teaching a classroom full of third graders and she suddenly thought her heart was breaking. She got somebody to take over her class and ran to the office and borrowed the phone.

The preacher, that meddling Presbyterian fellow, answered the church phone himself.

"You don't know me" she cried, and then proceeded to vent her unhappiness: "He's got himself feeling good and I'm as miserable as I can be!"

The minister heard her cry for help, heard

the catch in her voice, and gently invited her to come in and talk to him.

"WHEN?" she wailed.

"How about now ?" he asked.

A badly lit corridor led to the pastor's study at the back of the church, and as she stumbled along it, she saw the minister standing in the door, waiting for her.

She remembered: "He held out his hands and I fell against him and started bawling...all over his shoulder! I had never seen him before and there I was crying all over this perfect stranger!" The young woman then blurted out, "You have ruined my life!"

When she could gain her self-control and take a chair in the pastor's study, he let her spill out her grief and then patiently started talking to her. She has never forgotten the simple advice he gave her. First, he pointed out, she would not want to get married if it was not really right with the young man. Having talked to him, the pastor believed that he loved her and would come back to her, but until then she should accept his decision and wait.

"Be quiet about your feelings of hurt," he cautioned her. "Don't go telling other people about it. If you need to, go in your closet and scream. If you're mad at God about it, tell Him. But don't make a public issue of it."

And finally, the hardest of all to accept, "You're going to live. Things are going to be all right."

She left, somewhat mollified, obscurely comforted. But a month later she was driving home from school, and the hurt came rushing back. She pulled over to the curb and gave way to tears, crying aloud, "I can't stand it! I can't stand it!" It wasn't exactly her closet, and she didn't precisely blame God, but she vented her feelings, as privately as she could on a busy street. Somewhat calmer, she was at home grading papers when she heard a knock at the door.

The young man stood there. "I give up," he said. "Let's get married. Let's do it right away before I change my mind!"

The next Sunday they went to North Avenue Presbyterian Church and sat together in the front row of the balcony. The minister saw them from the pulpit, and he winked at them.

That was the beginning of an enduring thirty-five-year friendship between the lanky, dark-eyed man who was to become one of the country's best-known and most-successful developers, Tom Cousins, his merry, silver-haired wife, Ann, and Dr. Vernon S. Broyles, Jr., pastor of North Avenue Presbyterian Church.

Tom and Ann Cousins were married in Ann's home church in Auburn, Alabama, where her father was president of the university. They returned to Atlanta and joined North Avenue Presbyterian Church, where they have been strong supporters and active participants in the work of the church ever since.

"The first person to call on us when we got home from our honeymoon was Dr. Broyles," Ann remembers.

The young Cousinses were to learn what many Atlantans already knew — that the steady, compassionate man who, without really knowing them, took seriously the crisis in their love life, also took on the problems of the town and the region. The man who, as Tom said, "really talks to God," was the confidante and close friend of poor slum children as well as the intimate of powerful financial and civic leaders of the town, who had influence that in time extended across the world. He was, as many have said, not only the most loved but the most "listened to" Protestant minister in the region.

Oddly enough, Vernon Broyles had no particular desire to become a big-city preacher and to take up a ministry at one of Atlanta's oldest—and in times past—richest and most fashionable churches.

He was content to shepherd a flock of three hundred in the small cotton town of Canton, Mississippi. He even regarded being in Canton, a circumstance some people would call an accident or coincidence, as a "happening of the Lord." It was the kind of thing that he felt occurred with awesome frequency throughout his life.

He had spent a year at the German University of Tubingen and then had traveled in Egypt, Palestine, Jordan, and Turkey. He took the Orient Express to Europe, where he was to board a ship for America.

"My ticket home was from Bremerhaven," he remembered. "The trip was just another act of God's providence in my preparation for the ministry. When I got to Bremerhaven, I had eighty-five dollars left. I was headed home with no job, no money, and a concern as to what was next. When I went to my stateroom on the ship, the *Bremen*, I found a letter from the Rapidan, Virginia, church inviting me to come and supply the church until I found a permanent place. It's not hard to imagine how different this made my trip back home. God's strange providence!"

His father and stepmother, Martha, lived in Meridian, Mississippi, and he went to see them before beginning his stint at Rapidan. While he was visiting there, the Presbyterian church in Canton invited him to preach one Sunday. He was glad to do it and cheerfully accepted as compensation the contents of the offering plate, $6.42.

Back in Rapidan, he received a call from the Presbyterian church in Lumberton, North Carolina. Simultaneously there was a call from the Canton church. Maybe the size of that offering of $6.42 had something to do with it, but he decided to accept the invitation from Lumberton.

It was an offer, he recalled, that was "attractive in every way," and he headed for the telegraph office to notify the Lumberton Presbyterians that they had a new minister, and the Canton church that he regretted.

He remembered, "Between my parked car and the telegraph office was the post office. I stopped there. There was a letter from a Canton elder. In some strange way the letter changed my mind, and I reversed the messages to be sent. Why Canton? There was no detail not more attractive in Lumberton. I can only believe that the Lord wanted me in Canton."

Canton in the 1930s had a population of slightly less than five thousand people. In its one-hundred-year history, Canton was said by the WPA guide book to have achieved a character that was neither that of the Old South of the Big Black River valley nor that of the pine woods of the Pearl River valley, these being the two streams that frame it. It was regarded as having an "old prosperous and advanced culture," partly because its proximity to that famous old thoroughfare, the Natchez Trace, gave it a wealth that expressed itself in a large complement of white-columned mansions and half a dozen beautiful churches. Because it was in the center of Madison County, Canton was selected to be the county seat in 1835, when it was little more than a pretty village of big trees and bounding deer. It won out over the larger, older town of Madisonville which, according to contemporary reports quoted in Carol Lynn Mead's county history, was on the Natchez Trace near the house of Puk-shun-nubee, a Choctaw chieftain, and only about three miles from the Choctaw boundary and therefore "subjected to such dangers as might exist because of the hijackers and other outlaws said to have infested the Trace as well as not-so-gentle rivermen who took that route back to their northern homes after delivering boats and cargoes in New Orleans."

Canton was described by many as the prettiest village in "the southwest," and, as a traveler wrote in the *Mississippi Creole* in 1842, had the advantage of being "shut out of the din and turmoil of marts and dissipations that will intrude" on more populated places.

The First Presbyterian Church was established in the 1830s and met for fifteen years in the town hall or borrowed sanctuaries from other denominations. Its founding pastor died of yellow fever while traveling to Natchez as an evangelist, and his body is buried behind the church he helped to build. During the Civil War the pastor was away serving as a chaplain in the Confederate Army, and the church itself was used to quarter Confederate soldiers, who removed the metal pew markers and melted them down to use as bullets.

Vernon arrived to assume his new ministry in time to deliver the first sermon of January 1933. The church had been without a pastor for more than a year. He had expected to live in the church's manse, but the old house, long untenanted, was not in good repair and was neither comfortable nor attractive. He started looking around. An elder in the church, Jimmie Smyth, who was superintendent of education for the town school system and had been a member of the pulpit committee that selected him to come to Canton, suggested to the young minister that he find a boardinghouse. Smyth himself had just lost his own quarters because his landlady was giving up the boardinghouse field, and he was looking.

It was not unusual for the mistresses of the erstwhile stately homes of Canton to take in paying guests. They had spare rooms and usually superlative cooks in their kitchens. So the two bachelors had a choice of five or six prospective berths when they set out. One of their first stops was at the home of Mrs. Bena Virden, the widow of the town clerk and herself a member of the clerk's staff. That day the daughter of the household, also named Bena, who taught at Mississippi State College for Women in Columbus, was home for the weekend. She heard the men's voices in the living room and called out to Mr. Smyth, her old friend and teacher.

He walked back toward her room and she greeted him ebulliently. He regarded her as one of the brightest students he had ever taught in his years as a math and physics teacher, and she was so pretty and full of fun he delighted in seeing her.

"Tell your preacher friend," she whispered, "if you all come here to live you won't be bothered by this old maid."

A twenty-six-year-old old maid, scoffed Mr. Smyth, laughing at her. She would be an ornament to the premises and a delight to the tenants. But he and his friend were looking for a bit more room—a bedroom each and a study for the minister. They walked across the yard, through the garden of a big, white-columned house facing Fulton, the next street over, and rented the rooms they needed from Mrs. Virden's sister and her husband, Dr. and Mrs. James Priestly.

It was a charming house with cool, high-ceilinged, honeysuckle-scented rooms looking out on a quiet street and with a superb cook named Eula, who was dedicated to filling them with wonderfully nourishing meals. They moved in.

Vernon spent a lot of time studying when he wasn't busy with church affairs and the work of the Rotary Club, which both of the young men had joined. But Jimmie and other members of the household were amused to notice that he left the living room and front porch many evenings to stroll through the garden, and they did not think that he was gathering vegetables or flowers. It became apparent that the self-styled old maid in the house beyond was the attraction.

Bena Virden was enormously popular—a slender, laughing girl with a mop of dark curls gathered in a loose chignon on the back of her head, an incandescent smile, and a gift for playing the piano. Her musical ability had won top honors in state competitions, and she was therefore greatly in demand to play at meetings and parties. She had a big family connection and spent time visiting new babies and brides and old cousins with her mother.

A diary keeper in her early years, she was an adroit raconteur and a humorous observer of and participant in the tranquil life of the small southern town. History, particularly family history, was of enduring interest to these Old-South families, and when the town of Canton celebrated its one-hundredth birthday in 1934, Bena was as charmed as old aunts and cousins by yellow family portraits rounded up out of albums and musty trunks. When an elderly kinsman came to supper wearing his frayed Confederate Army uniform, she rejoiced with him in the possession of a button once worn into battle by that most revered (by southerners) and peerless General Nathan Bedford Forrest.

As a young teacher who knew something about drama, Bena was pressed into service to direct plays, advise the debating team, chaperon student outings, and cope with the backstage crises that arose when her young cousin starred in the fifth grade's operetta.

Bena loved her hometown and wrote often of its beauty. In 1934, she reflected on the awakening of spring in the cemetery: "Topsye's [her aunt, Mrs. Priestly] pear trees are budding and the redbud all over town will be in full bloom in a few days. The pansies on Daddy's and little Percy's [her younger brother who died in childhood] graves look like enormous bouquets. The whole cemetery is lovely. So many people have daffodils and hyacinths. Lillian Reid's grave is covered with the most beautiful violets I've seen. The big trees are budding and the mockingbirds have come back. The whole effect on me is one of peace and—intimacy. I sometimes feel it's the least lonely place in town. Four generations of us buried there—together, surrounded by families we've loved for a hundred years."

She wrote of spending a Sunday afternoon with an aunt who showed her letters exchanged between her grandparents when they were young and newly married. She was especially touched by her grandmother's letter which began: "My dear husband—what a satisfaction it gives me to use that word 'mine' in connection with you."

She went with friends to Mobile and New Orleans and Natchez and was pleased to meet in the famous antebellum Natchez mansion, Melrose plantation, ladies who knew Canton and had family connections there. She joined her mother in staging a small surprise party for Dr. and Mrs. Priestly on a wedding anniversary and there made her first mention of the family's preacher boarder. She was arranging coffee and cake in the upstairs sitting room when "Vernon came bounding up the stairs whipping out a handkerchief which

16

he offered me on his broad shoulder, his way of teasing me because Bob (a suitor) is not coming Easter. I tried to call his bluff by pretending to rest my curly head thereon but he didn't bat an eyelash and I had to back down."

The party was slow to get going, and she reported that her aunt kept the conversation "on my affairs," making her very uncomfortable because "Jimmie and Vernon must be bored to death hearing about me."

Vernon had acquired a secondhand Dodge, and he and Jimmie were to take Bena for a spin as she departed for home. She confided to her diary for the first time that she had been "longing for just such a setup" but it did not go well. She couldn't think of anything to say "and Vernon was much more interested in the Dodge than in me. So I was furious with him, too."

"When we came home I was extremely curt about asking them in—simply because I knew they were bored with me. And when Mother invited them in very cordially Vernon just turned pointedly to me and waited. And when my belated and feeble second came, he laughed at me and left. I could cry because I was so ungracious. What makes me act like that?"

Vernon's name appears with increasing frequency through the ensuing weeks. Sometimes she suspects some friend who talked of him a lot of setting her cap for him. Once she reported going with a date to his church on Sunday night and feeling a surge of sympathy at the presence of so few worshippers, eighteen adults and fourteen children: "I felt terribly sorry for Vernon. It must damp one's fire to face that pitiful handful. He discarded his sermon and made an impromptu talk on missions in Egypt, where he has traveled twice. Doug didn't think much of his talk but I liked it better than his usual Sunday night Bible story. For one thing, I believe intensely in missions. Besides, I am easily charmed by the glamour of foreign names...Port Said, Beyruth, Cairo."

The plight of a twice-married friend who wanted Vernon to perform a third wedding ceremony for her was very amusing to Bena. The young Presbyterian minister was opposed to marrying divorced persons unless it could be proved that they were the innocent parties in the divorce. He asked for an investigation into the divorces of the would-be bride, and the town waited to see how it would turn out.

Suddenly, to Bena's vast amusement, her friend Doug reported that Vernon had quickly and quietly performed the marriage ceremony and that the young couple was off to Miami on a honeymoon. But Vernon had not mentioned it at the house. Topsye could have killed him for being so secretive. They had to assume that Vernon did not feel good about the ceremony for the young woman, now three times a bride.

The minister's desire to keep the matter confidential was useless in a small town. The gossip finally got out that there had not yet been a second divorce and that the Reverend Mr. Broyles had finally agreed to officiate at the repugnant third ceremony because the couple was threatening to call on the town's Episcopal clergyman.

"Good heavens, not he!" Vernon was quoted as saying. He finally decided, according to Bena's friend Doug, that "one can do as much harm leaning too far backward as the other way." If and when the matter of the divorce decree was settled, he added, he would marry them. The divorce decree, obtained in faraway Dallas, turned out to be in order, and the young couple went to the church with two witnesses. Doug told Bena he would remember that brief wedding ceremony long after he had forgotten more elaborate, big-church ceremonies.

Bena had many men friends and a seemingly unending supply of escorts for parties, trips to town fetes, and the movies. Only once does an existing diary show how little they meant to her. "I know I'm selfish," she wrote. "I have so many blessings. But why can't I find somebody to love?"

Her mentions of the handsome neighbor, Vernon, are casual, with no reference to a growing interest on either side or a courtship. But within a few weeks she wrote, "Who would have thought I'd fall in love with a penniless divine?"

Bena Virden and Vernon Broyles were married in the Canton Presbyterian Church on October 9, 1935, with the minister from the Baptist church, where the Virdens were members, officiating. Jimmie Smyth, who was a groomsman, had persuaded them to use his new Dodge on their honeymoon trip to Virginia, leaving Vernon's old Dodge all tricked out in "Just Married" signs and shoes and tin cans in front of the Priestly house, where the reception was in progress.

The couple settled in happily in the Virden house, and Bena transferred her church membership to Vernon's pastorate. She had gone there many times, usually to weddings and special services. What she had perhaps not realized was that she, an unquestioning "cradle Christian" with a lifetime of church attendance and obedience to the doctrine of the church, would be intellectually stirred to probe the mystery of faith. She had learned the awesome thing that countless church-goers were to find later, that there was a depth beyond routine exposition of the scriptures in Vernon's sermons, that there was a quality of intense inner certainty that caused Tom Cousins to say years later, "He believed there was somebody up there! He was talking to God!"

Vernon wasn't exactly a "penniless divine" anymore. The church had raised his pay from one hundred dollars a month to three thousand dollars a year, and, with the Virdens' big house there to welcome them, life in the small Mississippi town at that time, if not affluent, was certainly comfortable and pleasant.

Their first child, a son, was born two years later, an occasion for celebration among such New Orleans friends as the famed lovelorn columnist, Dorothy Dix, who wired them that it was also the birthday of a distinguished Canton citizen, Captain James Dinkins, a man who rode with Nathan Bedford Forrest and was one of the oldest living Confederate veterans. They should name the new baby James Dinkins, decreed the New Orleans friends.

Too late, Vernon wired back. They had already named him Vernon Seba Broyles III but would be happy to give him the nickname, Cap'n, for the celebrated Confederate. To this day the younger Broyles, a Presbyterian minister in Louisville, Kentucky, is called "Cap" by his family and friends.

Cap was three and his sister, Bena, called Bebe, was eighteen months old when a group of well-dressed strangers showed up in their father's church one Sunday morning, listened attentively to his sermon but got away without introducing themselves after the service, which was customary. On their way home Vernon and Bena wondered about them, joking that they were obviously city people. A week or two later another man they did not know appeared and apparently endeavored to be inconspicuous. However, in that small congregation he was, as Jimmie Smyth said, as obvious as a department store detective on the trail of a shoplifter or, as Vernon said, a coal miner with his headlamp on.

They suspected that Vernon was being appraised by a pulpit committee from some city church. Sure enough, another group came and explained that they "happened" to be in the area and were looking for a small church for Sunday worship.

Vernon and Bena laughed together over that. There were smaller churches all up and down the 450-mile length of the Natchez Trace, many of them more historic and more picturesque than Canton's Presbyterian. This was apparently a group in Canton on a mission. Vernon then made a decision which was to guide him all his life. He would leave the outcome of this pulpit committee's search to God, neither seeking its approval nor any pastorate it might have up its collective sleeve.

In due course John K. Ottley, Sr., president of the First National Bank in Atlanta and an elder in North Avenue Presbyterian Church, called Vernon and explained the visits of the eight strangers. They were interested in him, very interested, but there were still some members of the church to be sold. He would like the young minister to come to Atlanta to be interviewed.

"Thank you," said Vernon politely, but

"No."

"Well, how about meeting us in Birmingham," suggested the banker, "that's halfway."

"No," said Vernon again. He then heard Mr. Ottley shout, "Praise the Lord! I've got 'em now!"

There was a handful of dissenters in the church, fearing that the Mississippi minister might be too liberal in his views on premillennialism, the belief that Christ's return will precede a millennium of the messianic rule foretold in Revelation. Since he had never seriously considered the matter, Vernon was not prepared to express a view. But he and Bena had decided that a firm call from the Atlanta church would definitely interest them.

On New Year's Day in 1941 they arrived in Atlanta with two little children, both suffering from colds and fever, and a black friend of Bena's family named Idonia, who had signed on as nursemaid for the trip and to get them settled in Atlanta. The church had reserved rooms for them at one of the better downtown hotels, the Ansley. The manager took one look at the party and murmured to Dr. Broyles that they could not accommodate black Idonia. The weary minister went across the street to the old Piedmont hotel. Same story. They drove out West Peachtree to the Biltmore. Idonia was not welcome. In the cold rain with darkness falling they made it back downtown and went to the Robert Fulton, a smaller, less than grand commercial hotel. Grudgingly, warning them that Idonia would have to remain out of sight in the room, the fourth hotel accepted them.

Exhausted, the minister marshalled his little family upstairs and to bed—fervently wishing that they were all back in Mississippi, a state not famous for liberal views on race but reliably cordial to any black servant.

*A merciful providence steered me through
the years with never failing ways I could not
have prepared or provided.*
VSB in his Journal

Vernon Broyles knew well what that lifelong Mississippian, William Faulkner, is cred-
ited with knowing about the alienation, the
rootlessness, and the despair that plagued the
human race. He, too, grappled with the ten-
sions of the times—war and racism and the
private and personal devils of the poor, the
church-going middle class, and a whole seg-
ment of the rich and powerful, who sought
his help and accepted his friendship and
counsel.

He had known few of the rich growing up,
this descendant of Tennessee farmers, and
he did not seek to become what the theological community in Atlanta later and with
amused affection called "Minister to the Moneyed," "Chaplain to Coca Cola."

As a child Vernon was so afraid of the dark his mother ran a cord from his bed to her room so he could tug on it and get comfort and reassurance from her when he awakened in the night. He was often lonely and ill at ease with the well-to-do youngsters who attended the private school where his parents enrolled him. He was at least temporarily snubbed by the college fraternity he wanted to join. He was broke and tormented by uncertainty when he finished college.

How then did he become the man who latched on to the minds and hearts of so many people, rich and poor?

The cliches of the pulpit were rarely heard from Vernon Broyles, and when he spoke of "God's providence" it was with a profound personal conviction that changed it from a theological conundrum to something as simple as bread, as miraculous as rain on the parched earth.

Over and over in the journal, which he kept through the years, he writes of the intervention of God in his behalf at crucial points and of the benevolence of God in the happy fulfillment of his personal life and in his mission as a minister.

With the patient frugality of the Scottish Presbyterian, he took the circulars and junk mail which came his way, carefully halved each page horizontally, and used the backs to write on in a tiny, ink-saving script that has strained the eyes of many a typist.

Even his sermon notes are inscribed in this infinitesimal script on the backs of form letters and financial reports from a variety of places and, to the astonishment of secretaries, who later prepared them for printing or for the newspaper column that he wrote for four years, he himself had no trouble reading them.

This journal points up an amazing fact to people who have through the years heard his sermons, called on him to lift them from the Slough of Despond, or felt his presence beside them in time of crisis. He never wanted to be a minister.

He wasn't exactly sure what he wanted to be, but despite his mother's deep spirituality and her insistence on religious training for him, he felt no call to the ministry.

His journal tells the story: "I was born in Rogersville, Tennessee. My father was an itinerant photographer and my mother was from a farm family in Parrottsville, Tennessee. Dad had a very limited education. Mother had some college. Dad's family were poor, a large family on a small farm. He left the farm when [he was] twenty-one years old to make his future with a sack of ham biscuits and $4.21 saved for him by his mother. In that poor boy was fixed ambition to find work other than farm labor. He bought a portable photographer's outfit used by itinerants to take pictures of various country gatherings. He shortly set up in Rogersville, Tennessee, where I was born. Six months after my birth the family moved to Knoxville to seek their future in more fertile fields. Here Dad got a job selling industrial life and accident insurance. Here began a career of some thirty years, this poorly prepared country boy 'making good.' Character and hard work took him up through the years to self-education and large managerial positions.

"My mother, Ella Mae Ellison, was from a family more financially stable. All seven children had college opportunities. There were one physician and two lawyers among her brothers. One, Uncle Thad, remained on the home place farm and was the greatest of all. He and his wife, Aunt Ethel, provided a home base to which the brothers and sisters and their children returned for extended visits through the years. My mother was a dedicated Christian, as were all her family. She shared the leadership genes of the family. She moved through difficult years and difficult situations, overcoming what she could and making the best of what she couldn't. She was a strong anchor for my life.

"My first five or six years were spent in Knoxville, where Dad began his career in the industrial life insurance business. For a relatively uneducated country boy to begin a successful career indicates the character and ability hidden there, which carried him through the years."

As young as he was, there's a Tom Sawyeresque quality in Vernon's memories of those days in Knoxville. He had only vague recollections of the birth—at home—of his baby sister, Elizabeth, beyond having been sent to spend the night with the next-door neighbor. But he remembered clearly falling down the steps to the cellar, where butter and milk were kept, and cutting himself on the shards of a cut-glass butter dish. He had the scar on his wrist to remind him all his life. He remembered that the streetcar went past their house and that he had an arrangement with the motorman whereby he could flag a ride to the end of the line a few blocks away and back again.

"There was a combination police and fire station two or three blocks away. I would go there to visit the men—to my delight, if not theirs."

His most vivid recollection was of the collapse of the stucco wall of the house where they lived under the onslaught of a rainstorm.

In 1910 Mr. Broyles was promoted to district manager in Grenada, Mississippi, "a remarkable evidence of his growth in every area," and the family moved there.

Vernon wrote of "scattered memories"— the neighbors across the street, going with his mother to see Haley's comet,"which I saw at its next appearance," and Sunday afternoon walks with his father, during which he saw an artesian well and a pair of oxen pulling a wagon loaded with logs.

"The church made its first imprint on my life," he wrote. "My mother must have 'joined' me to the church at six years old for I have no memory of ever joining. The minister was Dr. Caruthers, who[m] I remember as being very old, although he probably was not. Mother took me to church. Dad never went. It is still strange to me that I have no memory of contacts with my sister, a baby at the time."

Mr. Broyles continued to do well in his insurance business, and a couple of years later he was transferred to Mobile as manager of a large office. "Here a major part of my growing life was spent. Our first lodgings were in a boarding house run by a Mrs. Brewer. The house was on St. Louis Street in an old part of the city. She was the mother of Mrs. Leonard McGowin, whose husband was part of the 'establishment' in Mobile. As a child I had a desire to 'belong,' which probably came from my mother. She had ambition for herself and for her children to be a part of the community.

"Our lives in Mobile can probably be summed up as being conscious of this 'inner circle,' associating on its outer edges yet never really being a part of it. Mobile is an old town and its establishment is or was clearly defined and very hard for outsiders to penetrate.

"At Mrs. Brewer's I learned to ride a bicycle belonging to her grandson, bought chocolate cigars from an Italian fruit stand, was nearly badly hurt by tripping on a wire stretched across the sidewalk about six inches from the ground by some 'playful' soul. I went to school in a changing neighborhood school. It was frightening and I dodged contact where I could. I do remember learning the Alabama state song sung to the tune of the German national anthem.

"We soon moved to a house on Georgia Avenue, number 2539, I think. It was and is a very nice neighborhood. Strange to think of it now, we had a horse and buggy as our family conveyance. There were automobiles but also many horse-drawn vehicles. Fanny, the horse, was stabled in the backyard.

"On Sunday afternoons we went riding, Sister and I standing in the back with the top folded back to brace us. On Sunday at church there were automobiles parked but also some buggies and a surrey or two with fringed tops. My memories of the early years on Georgia Avenue are really few and scattered. I was timid and afraid of some of the boys on the street. Yet I took part in the play of the neighborhood. The family joined the Government Street Presbyterian Church soon after coming to town.

"At between ten and twelve years or a bit older I had a regular Saturday afternoon routine, going to the picture show to see such serials as "The Iron Claw" and "Perils of Pauline." My allowance was twenty-five cents. It took a nickel to ride the street car to town, a nickel to get in the picture show, a nickel for a bag of popcorn, a nickel to get home with, and a nickel left for Sunday school the next day. Sometimes I spent the extra nickel and walked the two miles home.

"I attended Leinkauf school through the seventh grade. It was a pleasant experience all told. I remembering being called out of third grade by my Dad to come out and tell Fanny, the horse, goodbye. She had been sold.

"The third grade teacher was an attractive young woman. She was probably twenty-three or twenty-four. She announced to the class that she was getting married. I wondered why an old person would want to marry.

"All my early years I was an avid baseball fan. Mobile had a team in the Southern League. I went quite often and usually walked the two or three miles home. I learned to walk through Magnolia Cemetery bravely since it saved quite a bit of distance. My mother was careful of her children and it has always seemed remarkable how she allowed me to venture out far and often without seeming alarmed about possibilities of harm.

"It seems strange that I remember so little in these years of family life and Dad's and Mother's relationships. Until 1915 Dad did not go to church, leaving it to Mother to take her two children faithfully.

"Some time along here the family moved around the corner to 1051 Elmira Street. This must have been about the time Fanny was sold for I remember our first car, a Buick, was associated with the Elmira house. Not long after moving to the house on Elmira Street I left home one Saturday morning to play with friends in the Spring Hill gullies. I'll never forget turning the corner and looking down the street and seeing the second-story window of our house was gone. The house had caught fire and was badly damaged. No one was hurt and we rented space while the house was being rebuilt. Dad bought it in its burned condition and we enjoyed having our own home when the reconstruction was finished. The undamaged furniture was stored and when Dad went to claim it, the nicest pieces had been stolen."

Despite this loss the years passed pleasantly for young Broyles in the old coastal city with its streets shaded by centuries-old live oak trees and its beautiful and serene gardens, where tea olive perfumed the air and azaleas and camellias heralded each spring with masses of bloom. His parents were steady, caring people who wanted the best for their children, and it worried them that young Vernon had not made good grades at Leinkauf. "A general drifting within myself," he called it.

Mr. and Mrs. Broyles decided on what was a major step many far wealthier Mobile families hesitated to take in those days. They removed Vernon from public school and enrolled him at University Military School, run by Dr. Julius Tutwiler Wright, scion of an Alabama family well respected in educational circles. (A building at the University of Alabama in Tuscaloosa bears the name of his mother.)

"The school demanded the best from the students in a well-rounded curriculum," Dr. Broyles wrote in his journal. "You recited in every class. If you missed two questions you got a 'deficient.' If you had two 'deficients' in one class or more than three in all your classes in a week you came back the next day at 7:30 in the morning, stayed until 6:00 that evening until you had made them up. The military regime added to the strict requirements with its precision training in conduct and discipline."

The Broyleses could ill-afford the school, but as they watched their son, handsome in the blue-gray school uniform, take his place in the smart ranks of Dr. Wright's cadets and plunge whole-heartedly into his studies, they felt that their financial sacrifice was well worthwhile.

The rule of the school was that students who were up in their work could leave at noon on Friday. Young Vernon, motivated as much by that tempting half holiday as by a zeal to learn, only missed a Friday on the rare occasions when illness put him behind in a subject. It was an influence that he valued all his life. "I learned to apply and discipline myself to meet each day's obligations as they fell due. Here God had moved in my parents and in me to prepare me for the opportunities of the future."

In later years Vernon would, as a minister, be outspoken against the Supreme Court ruling that prohibits Bible reading and prayer in the public schools, an attitude which was almost certainly born in Dr. Wright's school.

"There was a Christian commitment in

the school that was always in evidence in Dr. Wright and many of the teachers," he remembered. "Every morning the whole school met for a brief devotional led by Dr. Wright. He would quote a verse or two from the Bible and comment on it. I still remember many of the verses he used. The importance of a Christian framework in the education of young people was thus imbedded in me without my being aware of it. This most certainly bore results in my later part in establishing the Westminster Schools in Atlanta on a firm commitment to Christ providing the best possible education for young people."

Two notable friendships developed during Vernon's years at Dr. Wright's school. His friendship with a girl named Barbara Blacksher, member of an old and socially prominent Mobile family, continued through his sophomore year in college and through her marriage and until her death. The other significant friendship of those early years was with a fellow student named Armistead (Bill) Christian, a sustaining friend whose family offered him a second home when he badly needed it.

In the summers Mrs. Broyles and her children spent a lot of time in East Tennessee with relatives. "The center of these summers," wrote Vernon, " was Mother's home place, which her brother, Uncle Thad, had acquired through the years. He and Aunt Ethel maintained a center for all the scattered family summer after summer. There was a spirit of hospitality there that I have never seen equalled. Whoever came was welcome to stay as long as they cared to. We usually were there two months. Aunt Ethel was a wonder. We visited other relatives for short periods during those visits. Dad's sister, Aunt Julia, and Uncle Roland Painter also maintained a welcome station for any of the family who came.

"My life is full of memories of these summers and is what it is because of the experiences in them. On both sides of the family they were people of integrity and faith. The church played a part in their lives. All were hard-working folk. Some were fairly well to do, some were poor in this world's goods. Yet all were people of pride and hospitality. I found later in life that these contacts were basic in my learning that the financial standing of a person was far less important than what a person was. People are pretty much the same at whatever level financially, and poverty doesn't necessarily cause unhappiness and misconduct. They were all kind to me, a growing boy, and my memory is full of a large supporting cast for my development under the molding hand of God."

Fondly he calls the names of twenty or more relatives, including Uncle Bascom, who was mayor of Johnson City and who ran unsuccessfully for Congress, and Uncle Frank, who was a mail carrier, a Bible teacher, and a columnist for the county newspaper.

Family discussions of politics on the front porch loomed large in his memory and so did small details of daily living—the privy, carrying water from the spring, lamplight, trading eggs for candy at the country store, eating at a second or third table when company overflowed the big house, riding with his uncle on his mail route, working in a flour mill owned by another uncle.

It was a halcyon life for a boy, but it changed abruptly—and tragically — for young Vernon the year he was sixteen years old. He came home from school at lunchtime one spring day during exam week at Wright's. He intended checking the mail and getting back to school, knowing that his mother had planned to be at a luncheon meeting of the Woman's Club a few blocks away.

He was riffling through the mail when he

heard her moan. She lay unconscious on her bedroom floor.

Frantically he called the doctor and his father, and when the doctor didn't get there immediately he ran down the street to ask the help of a nurse they knew.

He was running back to the house when he saw his father standing on the steps.

"She has died," his father said.

It was a rough time for Mr. Broyles and his two children, but Vernon was to learn something then that stayed with him all his life. In his ministry he was famous for a kind of intuition which caused him to appear without having had notification—uncalled for, apparently uninformed and without having received any appeal for help—at a moment of deep grief or pain.

"I don't know how he knows," church members say of his mystifying appearances. "But you can set your watch. Within fifteen minutes after trouble hits you, Vernon Broyles is at your side."

Dr. Dunbar Ogden, pastor of Government Street Presbyterian Church, appeared at the

Elmira Street house almost before the doctor did. He prayed with Mr. Broyles and Vernon and Elizabeth and lingered beside them.

"He helped us to comfort and strength in a way never to be forgotten. Remembering his presence I have as a minister tried to be there to pray even if there is little else to do or say. I learned that it is not important what you say but it matters whether you go, whether you're there. One's presence penetrates the cloud of grief and what is said is secondary."

There was a funeral service at the church, and then they took Mrs. Broyles's body home to Parrottsville for another service and burial. Here Vernon, who later became known for his ability to tailor his sermons to radio time, ending them on the exact second the air schedule dictated, saw the opposite—the long, drawn-out service. In the custom of the country, four ministers spoke and the service ran nearly two hours. "I learned that length is not the measure of effectiveness," he remarked later.

It was decided that Elizabeth would stay with her Uncle Thad and Aunt Ethel for the coming school year, and Mr. Broyles and Vernon left for Mobile by themselves. They had a stopover in Morristown, Tennessee, and they went to hear the famed evangelist, Billy Sunday, who was holding a revival there. His director of music, Homer Rodeheaver, had chosen the ancient camp-meeting hymn, "The Old Rugged Cross." The Broyleses were deeply moved. "I can still hear it in memory," Vernon said.

Sad and bereaved, the man and the boy found the house too empty to bear. They tried their hands at cooking and gave it up and went out to eat. They finally sold the house and moved to a boardinghouse. Mr. Broyles found partial escape from loneliness in a transfer to the company's Meridian office. He again lived in a boardinghouse where new friends eased his heart's heaviness. Vernon was spared this move by his friend Armistead Christian's family. They invited him to live with them for his senior year at Wright's, rescuing him from the wrenching experience of moving to a new town for his last year of high school, "pulling up every root that supported my life."

"No one can project what would have happened if this invitation had not come," he said later. "The chances are that I would have never made anything of myself at all. I was insecure at best and without very strong inner resources. I can only say that I am convinced that my mother's prayers for her boy saved me at that juncture. The Christians were a strong family of strong people, dedicated Christians, members of Central Presbyterian Church. There was a younger brother, Murray, and a sister, Edith. They took me in as a member of the family. I continued my attendance at Government Street Presbyterian Church.

"They gave me support in all my interests and activities and lovingly made me more nearly what I should have been. I was in Meridian for Christmas and occasional weekends but it was all marginal. Dad got along all right as he made friends and his agency did well. But he must have been lonely. I am sure I was not much help for him and I regret this."

The matter of college had to be settled, and Vernon favored the University of Alabama. But Bill Christian and three of their other classmates had settled on the smaller Presbyterian college, Davidson, in North Carolina.

"At the last moment I more or less drifted into the decision to go there. Again the hand of the Lord had to be behind this because out of it grew other turns in the road that were important."

45

With Bill Christian as his roommate, his freshman year at Davidson went along fairly well except for some uncertainty about being asked to join a fraternity. When he learned that only about a third of the 245 freshmen would get bids from the five fraternities on campus, he didn't have much hope that he would make it.

He almost didn't. Sigma Alpha Epsilon considered him but took the precaution of writing the Mobile SAE alumni group about him. The alums wrote back that he did not rate a bid. In spite of this, the SAE chapter at Davidson rushed him and gave him a bid. He did not find out about his near miss until his sophomore year when, as fraternity secretary, he found the correspondence relating to him.

His mother's brother, Newell Ellison, a Washington attorney and head of SAE of the Province area, of which the Davidson chapter was a part, had written, making a strong recommendation for Vernon.

Fraternity membership might seem a small thing to some men but to Vernon it was confidence building. "A popular group believed in me and accepted me, an experience I had never before had, bringing together my scattered and insecure personality."

Still alone in Meridian since Elizabeth continued to live with the Parrottsville relatives, Mr. Broyles became friends with a widow from Huntsville, Alabama, who had lived in Mobile and worked at Gayfers. In Vernon's sophomore year, Vernon Broyles, Sr., and Martha Geron Goodlett were married.

"No man," said Vernon, "ever had a more devoted wife and she cared for him in a wonderful way until he died."

At age sixty-five Mr. Broyles retired from his company with very slim resources in "a very tight time." But a way miraculously opened. The Life Insurance Company of Virginia had acquired twenty-four houses in Meridian on foreclosed mortgages.

"A friend of Dad's met him on the street one day. He told him he was handling these houses but wanted out. He asked Dad if he would be interested in taking them over. Dad knew nothing about real estate but said he would. They worked it out. Somehow Dad got a license and was in business. Martha came into it with him. She was a superior business woman and became the dominant power from this point on.

"Then one day two government men came

47

to Dad from the Home Owners Loan Corporation, which had several hundred homes in that area of Mississippi. The depression was well on the way and people were losing their homes in large numbers. The men told Dad he had been chosen to represent the HOLC in servicing and selling the houses. It was something all the Meridian real estate people were competing for. Dad did not know of it and had not applied. They told him they had carefully screened all the companies and had decided the government would get the most honest intelligent work from him, a tribute to Dad's lifelong integrity. This was the real beginning of a successful business which gave Dad and Martha security for their future. Martha soon had the reputation of being the best real estate operator in town."

During this period, at Davidson Vernon had taken three years of pre-med and decided that medicine was not for him. He had had a pleasant, productive time in college, serving in the ROTC, working as business manager of the college paper, and selling shoes to help defray his expenses. He was elected to a leadership fraternity, and to his surprise and pleasure, SAE assigned him the job of shopping for the phonograph records played at the fraternity house.

Now and then the possibility of becoming a preacher stirred in his consciousness and he pushed it down. "That was one thing I did not want to do!" But what he wanted to do he knew not.

"I had turned away from pre-med and my last year for no reason I could define I took Greek. Future events proved I was being prepared for the ministry, Greek would be needed, and the Lord evidently put it on my agenda."

One of the outstanding friendships Vernon made at Davidson was with C.K. Brown, a young teacher who taught him math in his freshman year and with whom he stayed in touch through the years. Professor Brown was so certain Vernon was going to be a preacher that he promised him then he would see that he got an honorary degree of Doctor of Divinity one day—and he did.

Graduation, far from being a triumphant end and beginning, as the speakers said, was "a rather devastating experience," Vernon recalled. "It was the beginning of the most difficult year of my life. Here I was at the end of four years of college with no job and no training for any kind of career, I had no money and no open door into the future that I could see."

Back in Meridian, warmly welcomed by his father and stepmother, he started looking for a teaching job. "I found I was not qualified," he reported.

He did get a job working for a bank at fifty dollars a month and that was a short-term career. His father offered him a job collecting on an insurance debit route and selling insurance.

"To put it simply, I was miserable. The call within me to the ministry began to press. I spent a good deal of time with the Bible. My social life was not bad. Dad and Martha were understanding but I could see no light ahead."

A good paying job with U.S.F.G., a big insurance company, came up and Vernon gave every evidence of excelling at it. His superiors were pleased with him, and his father was relieved that he had finally found himself.

It was the year 1928 and it seemed certain the job would provide him with the money and the sense of fulfillment that had eluded him. He hated it.

"The roof fell in—inside of me! I knew suddenly I had to go into the ministry."

He left for Union Theological Seminary in Richmond that fall—with the blessing of and a bit of financial help from his boss at U.S.F.G.

It is with a thorough feeling of humility that I accept this call to be the minister of this church....I do so with the promise to God and to the congregation of North Avenue Presbyterian Church that I will do everything within my power by work and prayer to make me worthy to be used of God's power and grace in your church and in our community.

VSB—Letter to Session, 1941

The Broyleses settled in a rented house at Park Lane and The Prado, an Ansley Park address not far from the small white two-story house that they would buy a year and a half later for $7,250.

Vernon had not been in the old church, and he went right away to inspect it and to get his bearings. His first impression was of drabness, dark curving pews, dark carpet, poor light. And then he glanced upward at the stained glass windows.

Five of them are Tiffany windows. Blazing shafts of light poured through the richly colored glass, illuminating the dim sanctuary in glowing color, which lifted his spirits and took his mind off the somber atmosphere.

A circular window, given in 1900 by Walker Inman and Mrs. Clem Harris showed young Jesus in the temple. The inscription "Wist ye not that I must be about my Father's business?" may have struck him as personally prophetic. He looked at the others: Jesus with a shepherd's crook in his hand and a lamb in his arms with the inscription: "I am the Good Shepherd"; a circular representation of Jesus surrounded by little ones and the inscription: "Suffer the little Children to Come Unto Me."

He stood long moments in admiration before he turned and went back to the study to finish preparing the sermon that he would have to deliver in three days.

"I don't remember what I preached," he said afterward. "I just remember being nervous. Dr. Flinn had always worn a cutaway coat and striped trousers and I went to be fitted for the same. It was the first time I had ever seen a cutaway coat. At Canton I had preached in a business suit. It was communion Sunday and there were twenty-eight elders—a crowd!—to assist with the service. At Canton I had managed with five. The church was filled with folks—all simmering with curiosity. Boy, it was a multitude!"

Vernon's formal installation came a month later with Dr. Flinn's son, Richard, one of three clerics officiating.

By then he had begun to take hold of the job in a way that would ever be his strength. He set out to know, really know, his congregation. The church had no staff beyond a secretary and Mrs. Helen Johnson, daughter-in-law of one of the partners of a famed department store, Chamberlain, DuBose and Johnson, which preceded Macy's by half a century. She was a gracious "old Atlanta" woman who had been a poised and cultivated hostess before the family business was sold, and she brought these talents to her job as church visitor. She knew all the members of the congregation and all about them. Dr. Broyles said, "She steered me like a pilot does a ship."

When relationships were "tricky" she warned him in time to save him from hurting feelings or making a personal faux pas. Before he came to Atlanta, one of the town's most sensational murders had involved the grandson of prominent North Avenue members. Both the young men were college students. One was married to a beautiful, musically talented girl who came regularly to church with his grandparents while her husband was in prison. She learned that a pianist was needed for Sunday school and she offered her services. Mrs. Johnson warned Dr. Broyles that he should proceed with caution before accepting her offer. He took the matter up with the elder in charge of Sunday school, a robust, out-spoken character named Homer Carmichael.

"Go ahead and get her," the elder said sturdily. "If anybody complains refer them to me."

Somebody did complain.

"What do you mean letting the wife of a murderer play the piano for our children?" they demanded.

"Homer Carmichael said if there were any questions they should be taken up with him," Dr. Broyles said.

Mr. Carmichael was daunting enough that the matter was dropped and the young woman played the piano for the Sunday school for many years.

The thirty-nine people who had voted against calling Vernon to the church were to be won over, and Vernon set about getting acquainted with them and ultimately enjoying their friendship if not their total approval. His predecessor, Dr. Flinn, and Mrs. Flinn had tactfully left the country on an around-the-world trip to make the young pastor's settling in easier. After they returned and when critics would take a grievance to Dr. Flinn about some innovation of the young "whippersnapper," the older minister would say cheerfully, "Isn't that wonderful? I've been wanting to do that for years!"

There were no immediate innovations. Vernon continued to follow Dr. Flinn's example in the cutaway coat, which he didn't like, until one of the senior elders, John Brice, died. Then he switched to an academic robe.

"I couldn't do that while Mr. Brice lived," he said. "He was so Presbyterian he would have considered a robe...," he laughed, "I don't know, probably Catholic."

Dr. Flinn's sons, Dick, a fellow alumnus from Davidson, and Bill, later a professor at Georgia Tech, and Bill's wife, Elizabeth, were very supportive. Dr. Flinn's wife, the former Anna Emery, a pretty and witty woman, who after fifty years of marriage still called her husband "Dr.Flinn," withheld judgment. She wasn't to be easily sold on the newcomer, but she was outwardly gracious and did not admit her doubts until Vernon had been on the job some months. He invited Dr. Flinn to join him in administering communion one Sunday, and after the service Mrs. Flinn told Vernon she had come around, she approved of him. Until her death she was a regular at North Avenue services and once, upon leaving the balcony, where she often sat, was heard to remark, "Best preacher I ever heard...best sermon I ever heard."

Vernon couldn't have disagreed more. He had heard great preachers. He had read all the sermons of stunning literary magnitude. He did not consider himself in that league. He took the word "minister" in its literal sense—to care about people and to serve them. He worked diligently on his sermons, spending hours in study, but those afternoons when he went forth to get acquainted with his flock laid the foundation for the feeling that would prevail among hundreds of Atlantans for the rest of his life. He was a true shepherd. He guided and tried to guard all of the members of his congregation. Their trials and triumphs became his in a very personal way. "He cared about me! He was there when I was in trouble!"

Mrs. Johnson was responsible for one of his innovations. She directed him to the downtown workplaces of many men of the church. He went to call on them.

"At that time," he said, "nearly everybody worked downtown and I could see and talk to fifteen or twenty people in one afternoon. It meant a lot to me and, I think, to them."

It must have been so because the congregation on any Sunday was heavily masculine, and as Paul Duke, a successful Atlanta businessman and a powerful North Avenue supporter, was to say, "It's a man's church."

The time-worn cliche about religion and church attendance being "in my wife's name" didn't apply here. Of course in those days only men served as deacons and elders, but they also sang in the choir, taught Sunday school, and pushed through any project in which the church became involved.

They were also off-duty friends of the minister, going to football and baseball games and playing golf with him. They welcomed him into the Rotary Club, where for years he was the sole Protestant minister. One of his best friends was Bobby Dodd, "the tall Tennessean" who became the famed football coach and athletic director for Georgia Tech. Bobby had really married into the church when Alice Davis, daughter of long-time members, became his wife. Dr. Broyles didn't like to miss a Tech game and he was not offended by the slightly heretical Tech slogan "In Dodd We Trust."

He was to extend his ministry to the big university four blocks away by launching programs aimed at including the away-from-home students in church activities and making them acquainted with other young people. Eventually the church acquired a special minister to students.

Vernon continued to devote part of most afternoons to visiting. After he had come to know most of the men, he went to their homes to meet the women and children. "It was a day when people stayed home more and you didn't have to phone ahead and make an appointment to catch them in. They were there and usually glad to see you."

Looking back later, he said, "I suppose I preached well enough to keep the machinery going. But God gave me a gift for making friends as well as dreaming a dream and selling it."

Vernon did not claim any skill in counselling. When he arrived in Atlanta there was, so far as he knew, only one psychiatrist in town, and the practice of going to an expert with one's mental and emotional problems had not caught on.

Yet he put in hours talking to troubled people, times which scores of people remember as guidance. "He helped me change my life," an Atlanta business leader said recently. "I was in deep trouble. My marriage was falling apart. My wife and I were on the verge of divorce but we had two small children. I didn't know if I had the right to break up their home. I was in agony over it and I went to see Dr. Broyles. In the end we stuck out the marriage until our children were almost grown and old enough to handle it."

Did the minister tell him what to do? "I don't remember that he was that specific. We talked. He prayed with me. He really cared what happened to me and my family. I joined his church and went regularly and came to my own conclusion."

Another man, third-generation head of a major Atlanta corporation, was in a similar quandary. His family were lifelong members of another church, but he had dropped out in his youth and considered that he had no church affiliation. He knew Vernon well and had always felt in the minister a quality of compassion and wisdom that he wanted to draw on. He went to see him but he couldn't bring himself to reveal the depth of his problems with alcohol. "I was not worth bothering about," he said. "I was no damned good."

Tortured, he wandered away, but one Sunday he slipped into the church and sat down in the back. "I hoped nobody would notice me. I don't think anybody did—but Vernon did. He passed by on his way to the vestibule to shake hands with the departing congregation. He saw me and looked into my face and whatever he saw there, he stopped and whispered, 'Come on back to my study. I'll be there in a few minutes.' "

It wasn't long before the man moved his hitherto unused membership to that church, and it wasn't long until he felt strengthened in his family relationships and restored to his position of leadership in the community. He was to become a generous contributor to North Avenue's expansion and to many of its projects.

Paul Duke grew up in North Avenue church's Sunday School. His mother and father had married in the church just before World War I and had separated when Paul was fourteen. Despite his parents' separation, young Paul's ties to North Avenue Presbyterian Church continued. He was not only Dr. Flinn's paperboy, but his mother was active in the church and taught a Sunday school class.

By the time Dr. Broyles arrived at North Avenue, Paul Duke had been without a father for several years. He had a reputation for working hard and playing hard, and was on the verge of dropping out of Boy's High when overtures of friendship — "just friendship, not an effort to preach to me or convert me" — came from Dr. Broyles.

As their friendship developed, Paul settled down, graduated from Boy's High, and went on to attend Georgia Tech, where he was an All-American center for the "Yellow Jackets" football team.

Paul graduated from Georgia Tech with two engineering degrees, and he went on to become an important Atlanta real estate entrepreneur and developer as well as a major influence in both North Avenue Presbyterian Church and the city of Atlanta.

Paul's change from high-school playboy to a responsible and productive church and community leader he attributes to the influence of Vernon Broyles. "I was only one of many teenagers who experienced the love of Vernon Broyles....Outside of the Bible itself I have never known, or heard of, anyone with Vernon's absolutely amazing ability to know so many different women, men, and children of all types and backgrounds and to help meet their individual needs. He, somehow, would always show up, or at least be available, to literally hundreds of us.

"My own desperate needs ended by my really idolizing this man of God as a teenager, and his influence continues to this day. I miss him deeply."

Vernon, himself, discounted any skill at counselling. He simply saw in every human being a certain divinity. Each person, rich or poor, good or bad, is a child of God, he affirmed, "precious with unending hope and worth limitless care." With the Old Testament prophet Jeremiah he heard the words of the Lord: "Before I formed thee in the belly, I knew thee, and before thou came forth out of the womb I sanctified thee."

The view, firmly held in the church, that Vernon had a special intuition about the griefs and pains of people in his care was arrived at early in his ministry. A young mother had a grievously ill child at Crawford Long Hospital a block away from the church. She was present when the doctor, diagnosing her child's condition, instructed a young nurse about medication. She listened carefully and, knowing something about drugs, was appalled when the nurse brought a different medication.

She protested that it was not what the doctor had ordered. In fact it could be dangerous. The nurse, a young beginner, brushed aside her questions, assured her that she knew better than the mother what the doctor had prescribed and started to administer the drug.

Just as the mother, on the verge of hysteria, started to physically restrain the nurse, Dr. Broyles walked in. Quietly but firmly he sent the nurse away, insisting that she go and find the doctor at once.

The mother was right.

"My child could have died," she said. "How did Dr. Broyles know to come at that moment?"

He said only, "I was in and out of Crawford Long hospital a lot. I suppose God guided me to that room. I didn't know one of our members was there."

Jack Etheridge, a well-known Atlanta lawyer, a former legislator and a former Superior Court judge, grew up in North Avenue, the son of one of the church's founding families. His father, also a Superior Court judge, was a close friend of Dr. Broyles. Asked if Vernon had a prescient knowledge of his father's illness and death, Judge Etheridge said simply: "I don't know. He was there with us when Dad died at 3:30 in the morning. He had been there all night. I don't know how he knew."

Much later after Tom Cousins, the young man who was reluctant about getting married, had become one of the nation's most successful developers, seven of his employees were returning in his private plane from a business trip to Vermont. The plane disappeared over Lake Champlain and could not be found. All of the passengers were presumed to be lost in the ice-locked lake. Tom rushed to the search scene. His wife, Ann, left at home with their children, was distraught with worry and grief for the seven friends she had known.

"It was a disaster," she said. "I knew I should go to the families of those men but I couldn't budge. I was paralyzed and numb. Suddenly Dr. Broyles appeared.

"I don't know how he knew. Maybe it was on the radio or television. I don't know. But he came. He prayed with me and he said we had to go at once to see those families. He drove me to their homes. I couldn't have done it alone, but he was right. Being there with them was not much but the best I could do."

It was Vernon's policy to stand at the door to the Sunday school building every Sunday morning and greet, usually by name, the children as they arrived. It was a good way to get acquainted, he said, and it made children more comfortable about facing the minister later in church. He was already a friend.

Ann Cousins found that the adults, a mother, for instance, could lose a bit of status at such times. One Sunday she had dressed her little boy with loving care, insisting that he wear the new saddle oxfords that matched his little suit, instead of the tennis shoes, which he loved. He howled protest after protest but she insisted, and when they got to North Avenue he was red-faced and still sniffling and fighting tears.

"What's the matter, Tommy?" Dr. Broyles asked, taking his small hand.

Tommy caught his breath and came out with a roar: "Why does God care if you wear tennis shoes to Sunday school?"

"God," intoned the minister with a twinkle in his eye, "does not care if you wear tennis shoes to Sunday school!" He turned to Ann and said, "It's your mother who cares what you wear to Sunday School!"

A teenager worked hard trying to "baby-sit out" a highly desirable (to her) ninety-nine-dollar "Cloud Nine" coat instead of the plain eighteen-dollar wool coat her family could afford. With the loving help of her mother and her siblings, they pulled it off. The day before Christmas the bill from layaway was marked "Paid" and the mother went home proudly bearing the big coat box.

It was an extravagant expenditure for that family and the most sumptuous gift any member had ever had. There was great jubilation when its owner awakened to find it hanging by the fireplace on Christmas morning. She was going to wear it to the carol service at the church and she fully expected that it would rock that citadel of worship with its magnificence and draw the envious eyes of all the worshippers.

Nobody noticed the coat.

Scripture was read, hymns were sung, prayers were said, and the members of the congregation smiled and filed out, wishing one another a merry Christmas. Not a word was said about the coat...until the family reached the front steps and paused to speak to the minister.

Dr. Broyles smiled and shook hands and gently smoothed the sleeve of the "Cloud Nine."

"Beautiful," he murmured. "It's a beautiful coat, Susan."

The young girl's day was made. The magic of Christmas was reborn. She wore the coat until she went off to college and then she slept under it. But how did Vernon Broyles know that a really kind of tacky ersatz garment was so important, so altogether breath-takingly wonderful?

Instinct, say those who knew him, Vernon Broyles instinct.

*If a poor man named Jesus
should come to this church...*
VBS to a committee

All churches probably have a cadre of founding families who want to keep the congregation free of poor people and sinners and persons with dingy, ungenteel problems. North Avenue Presbyterian was no exception.

Some relative newcomers to the church had a brain-damaged child. They knew two other parents with the same problem, and they sought out Dr. Broyles to ask if those three and others in the same boat might bring their children and meet in one of the church rooms and set up a clinic and exercise group, sharing neurological expertise where it was to be found.   Dr. Broyles immediately welcomed them and assigned them to one of the bigger Sunday school rooms.

The group grew and flourished and presently needed a copying machine to provide helpful material for distribution to all parents with the same problems. Someone contributed the machine, but right away a staff member raised an objection. It had no business being in a Sunday school room, she said. It took up valuable space and was unsuitable.

Dr. Broyles heard the objection and nodded amiably.

"Put it in my office," he said, much to the chagrin of the staffer.

A little later a longtime member looked at the group of parents and brain-damaged children and asked icily, "Are these people Presbyterians?"

The sister of one of the little girls smiled sunnily.

"Oh, of course," she said. "All brain-damaged people are Presbyterians!"

When he heard about it Vernon threw back his head and laughed heartily.

But snobbery in the church wasn't always a laughing matter. Once at a meeting of the church's public relations committee, a longtime, generously contributing member raised the question of the group called "Miss Pauline's children."

Miss Pauline Dennis, a retired Latin teacher, had at age seventy-two launched a one-woman missionary program among the poor children in the downtown area, many of them neighbors to the church. She provided clothes and shoes and haircuts for the young ones, brought them to Sunday school in cars driven by volunteers she recruited, and arranged dental care and campships for them.

Inevitably some of their parents started showing up at church, shabby and poor but resolutely putting their best Sunday foot forward.

The public relations committee member was dismayed.

"It's fine for those people to go to church," he said, "but do they need to come to THIS church? There are others they could attend where they might feel more...well, more comfortable."

Before his fellow committee members could think of anything to say, Vernon Broyles spoke from the doorway.

"If a poor man named Jesus came to this church," he said thoughtfully, "would we send him to another church?"

The committee meeting adjourned. The abashed snob said no more.

The Reverend Cook Freeman, who served as associate pastor at North Avenue for twenty-five years—from 1957 to his retirement in 1982—says that Vernon Broyles "knew more about running a church than any man alive" and was so knowledgeable about finances that he could have become a very wealthy man if he had chosen a business career. Business leaders admired his acumen, but what impressed his congregation was that he did not push monetary problems on them from the pulpit. He believed that it was a time for spiritual concerns, and he declined to nag about money on Sunday morning.

"If the need is there, it will be taken care of," he often said.

Warring factions sometimes sprang up in the church and Vernon, undismayed, handled them with consummate diplomacy.

"Sometimes they kept on being mad at each other but they were never mad at Dr.

Broyles," Mr. Freeman said. "He could usually calm them down and make them friends again."

In one instance he is remembered as deflecting angry criticism directed at himself. At a meeting of the elders, one gentleman took the minister to task for having spent church funds to attend a meeting of the World Council of Churches. It was an unnecessary trip and expensive, he pointed out.

"He really threw the book at Dr. Broyles," said the associate pastor, chuckling at the memory. "Vernon heard him out and when he had finished Vernon looked around the room and said pleasantly, 'Any questions?' There were none. 'Meeting's adjourned,' he said, and he and his critic left arm-in-arm."

Vernon never thought much about money for himself. He had led church members and community leaders to raise millions for missions and education and innumerable charities, but he was content for himself and his family to live simply.

"He would have loved to have had a purple Cadillac convertible," said his longtime friend, Dr. Finch, "but he had sense enough not to buy one."

Costly vacations were beyond the Broyleses. For years the month of August was for them a time spent in an old mountain cottage at Blairsville, borrowed from Mr. and Mrs. Guy Woolford, wealthy but unpretentious members of the church. Here Bena prepared their meals on a wood cookstove, the children ran free in hills and creek bottoms, and Vernon studied and planned for the coming year.

One memorable year he and Bena were able to take a trip to Europe. They stopped off in New York for a day or two to visit former longtime North Avenue friends Henry and Martine Joyner.

A reliable means of entertaining for them was a drive around Manhattan Island. "I'll never forget how interested Dr. Broyles was in all those big apartment buildings," Mrs. Joyner remembered. "He kept looking up at them and then we found out what was fascinating him. 'I wonder', he said, 'where they put their garbage.' "

Bena, the elder daughter, usually called Bebe, said she considered their family comfortable financially until she went to private Westminster School, which her father was instrumental in getting built and which was attended principally by the children of the affluent.

"Some of those girls had closets full of shoes!" she recalled, laughing at the memory. "We never thought beyond two pairs, one for every day, one for Sunday. I was amazed and I'm afraid I coveted all those shoes in spite of what Mother and Daddy had taught us."

Bebe's father had been saved from penury as a seminary student by one of those strokes of happy fortune he believed was the intervention of God. He had arrived at Union Theological Seminary in Richmond from Mississippi on a foggy, rainy day. His mood was as morose as the weather when he checked into a bleak dormitory room. Two days later he met a fellow student who was in a quandary, seeking somebody, anybody, who could help him out of a commitment he had made to Dr. Mack, a professor. A job with another professor had come up and it appealed to him more. He wanted to take it and he needed Vernon to tell Dr. Mack and maybe substitute for him as the professor's assistant.

Vernon didn't mind explaining his friend's defection to the professor but he had no idea that he could substitute for him. He could type but he did not know shorthand, and it was plain that the professor wanted somebody who could take dictation.

"Let's try it," suggested Dr. Mack.

It became more than a job. It was an introduction to the embracing warmth of a large, interesting family. The Macks invited Vernon into their home and recruited him to drive them on short trips around the beautiful Virginia countryside, including weekend stays at their summer home near Orange, Virginia. He went to parties and played a lot of bridge, but he wasn't happy.

"I felt I was where I ought to be but was lost as to how it would work out. My first months I played lots of bridge, went to parties and still felt lost in so far as direction was concerned."

One day Dr. Mack said, "You are having a hard time adjusting, aren't you?"

They talked and the older man made a suggestion that almost became a formula in Vernon's counselling with troubled people: "Read your Bible an hour a day and go to church somewhere every week for two months and you may find your answer."

"Desperate enough to try anything, I did this and in the course of the months the bridge and parties fell by the wayside," he reported. "The discipline of classes, study, and seminary life became attractive and my sense of direction came into focus."

Rapidan, Virginia, a beautiful little village, was but two miles from the Macks' weekend cottage, and it had a small Presbyterian church where seminary students were engaged to preach twice a month during the winter and full time in the summer.

"After my second year at the seminary Dr. Mack got me this place. I was there two summers, living in a guest house of the Macks." At the end of the regular three years at the seminary five graduate fellowships were awarded. The competition was strong since we had an unusually able class. Through Dr. Mack's influence I received one of these, which I took at Union for one year. In this fellowship year the Macks had me in for my meals. Dr. Mack talked to me about studying abroad a year."

The free meals, the income from the Rapidan church, and his fellowship, if properly saved, would pay for most of his expenses, Dr. Mack pointed out.

"That year I spent very little money," he recalled.

A lecturer on archeology came to the seminary that year, and he revealed that he was financing a "dig" in Palestine the next summer, which Dr. W. A. Albright, the foremost authority on that part of the world, would be directing. Dr. Mack promptly pushed forward Vernon and another student named John Bright to serve on the staff the next summer.

The "dig" took two months, and during the rest of the summer Vernon went to Palestine, France, Switzerland, Italy, Hungary, Alexandria, Cairo, and Jerusalem. He cherished all his life a book by his mentor on excavating Kirjath Sopher's ten cities.

He travelled across Turkey on the Taurus Express and boarded the glamorous Orient Express to travel to Tubigen, Germany, unable to speak the language but determined to learn. Again he was short of money, figuring that he could spend only 118 marks a month for lodging. Excited to be there at all, he didn't mind the "grim" second-class boarding house that was available to him.

"Then there happened one of those

strange turns of God's providence which made my months there a totally rewarding experience," he remembered.

"Charley McRae, a friend from the seminary, had been there for some months. He was living in the home of a Professor Von Huene of a noble but impoverished family, and so he took in students. His friend, Frau Thierfelder, took a foreign student into her home from a different country each year. She was looking for an American that year. Professor Von Huene told her of me at Charley's suggestion and she accepted me after an interview. She was the daughter of the minister of justice under the kaiser in the old empire, a true Junker aristocrat.

"Her large apartment was furnished from the palace in Berlin, where she grew up. I had probably the only room with a private bath for any student in Germany. I asked the price and she replied three hundred marks a month. I thanked her and told her my funds were too limited to enable me to pay that amount. She asked me how much I could afford to pay. I replied 110 marks. That would be acceptable, she said.

"She took an interest in me, got me included in many invitations into the homes of her friends, took me to concerts, and included me in her family circle. I became good friends with her son, Rudolf, who was teaching law in Kiel University, a seaport city in West Germany. We corresponded fairly regularly before our country entered the Second World War. Bena sent packages of food and articles women like to the Thierfelder family before and after the war. Rudolf was in charge of the justice department."

His time in Europe over, Vernon came home to an uncertain future. His friends, the Macks, were once more the source of support and warm hospitality. He lived in their guest house and preached parttime at the little Rapidan church. The call to Lumberton, North Carolina, came, and, just as he was prepared to accept it, something (he calls it the hand of God) propelled him to decline and accept instead a call to Canton, Mississippi, where he had received the paltry offering of $6.42 the summer before.

"They were good years," he wrote of the time in Canton. "I had opportunity to spend the necessary time in study and preparation of my doctor's thesis, the residence requirement having been met. During the first two years I wrote a history of the church's one hundred years—1835 to 1935. It was a valuable seven years in learning to live in a small town with all the currents that run through one. With local elections every two years, city and county, feelings could go high.

"The church never grew much but it was stable during those years of severe depression. The high point, of course, was my marriage to Bena Virden in 1935 and the births of a son, Cap, in 1937 and a daughter, Bena, in 1939. [Those were] seven satisfying and valuable years for me and, I trust, for the church.

There were opportunities to move during these years but none that had any sense of call in them."

Then came the appearance of strangers at a series of Sunday services. Dr. Richard Orme Flinn, the founding pastor of North Avenue Presbyterian Church in Atlanta and its guiding genius for forty-one years, had retired. The church he thought he had built in an almost rural area at the edge of the city, had become a downtown church with the old homes and gardens that lined Peachtree Street giving way to commerce—a bank on the corner, Kampers, a big charge-and-deliver grocery store, across the street, the Georgian Terrace Hotel, and the opulent Egyptian-style Fox Theatre a block away. The Erlanger Theatre was two doors away, a fire station less than a block away, and the Epicopal, the Methodist, and a towering Baptist church within view.

When Dr. Flinn picked the site for the city's newest Presbyterian church, he was criticized for choosing one "so far out in the country." He said he had thought about it carefully and visited the big wooded lot many times. He had seen buggies and carriages pass that way to Sunday outings at Ponce de Leon Park, a mile away. He decided, he said, that "if you're going to fish, go where the fish are."

The "fish" who joined him to found the new church came principally from the two downtown Presbyterian churches, First and Central. They came with the blessing of the older churches, which were, in that year of 1898, crowded. There was only one other church near the new location—a Methodist mission on Merritts Avenue, members of which, like good neighbors, extended to "our brethren our most cordial welcome," offering the use of their building "so long as the Presbyterian congregation may find it convenient or necessary." North Avenue was later able to return the hospitality when the Methodists built handsome St. Mark Church at the corner of Peachtree and Fifth in 1902-1903.

By 1939 when Dr. Flinn retired, the city had grown northward, far, far beyond the church, and rooming houses and slum landlords had encroached from the south and east. But North Avenue members, many of them the town's business and civic leaders, many of them wealthy, hung on, commuting weekly and sometimes daily from distant homes in the new northside area. They were determined to keep their church with its traditions a viable force in the life of their city. So they looked for a successor to Dr. Flinn, a hopeless task, many of them believed. There would be no replacing the venerable minister of whom, Dr. William R. Crowe, a church member and sometimes poetizer, wrote, "This good man for many years has held Atlanta by its ears."

They searched. A committee headed by John K. Ottley, Sr., president of the First National Bank, had a list of possiblities, and for eighteen months the pulpit committee traveled and looked and listened. A young man in Canton, Mississippi, was seventy-third on their list.

Vernon considered himself the remotest of their choices. "How many mainline churches go to a small Mississippi town and call a man just turned thirty-six with no track record?" he marvelled. "Then there was a controversy in the church from a strong minority over premillenialism (an old-fashioned church debate over the coming of Christ for a thousand-year reign.) One of them wrote me a letter asking my views. Frankly I never thought about the question. I answered as generally as I could."

Mr. Ottley's committee was sold on the young minister and prevailed. On February 9, he was installed as the second pastor of North Avenue with Dr. Flinn's son, Richard, a Carrollton minister, one of three clerics officiating at the installation.

Ten months later Vernon and Bena were having Sunday dinner with Air Corps General and Mrs. Troup Miller, members of the church, when the news came crackling over the radio: Pearl Harbor had been bombed.

"General Miller moved so fast I often wondered if he didn't make it to Washington almost as fast as we got back to our house in Ansley Park. I don't know how he got airborne so fast. We went by the church and I looked up at the belfry and wished that we had a bell to toll. I grew up hearing church bells ring in a little East Tennessee church of fifty people in the summertime. I don't remember why North Avenue did not have a bell, but I determined then that we'd get one when we could and, hopefully, ring it when peace was declared."

Vernon did not get his bell until after the war. Newspapers reported on December 22, 1954, that the church had brought the "aural and visual impact" of a bronze bell—a "new and mighty church bell" to Atlanta. It had been cast by the Royal Van Bergen Bell Foundries, makers of bells in Holland for 150 years, and was to ring thereafter at all worship services, calling people to prayer at noon every day and to weddings and other special events at the church.

Despite the war the Broyleses soon were able to purchase a house. A small two-story white Dutch colonial house in Ansley Park came up for sale for $7,250. Vernon borrowed the money and bought it.

"It wasn't much of a house," Vernon said, "but the location was fine. It was on the Prado, near McClatchy Park and was pleasant. We raised a family in it."

They had inherited most of their furniture from Bena's mother, and the movers were appalled to discover how heavy and unwieldy these antiques were. The church was paying them, and they doubled their original estimate when they finished wrestling with a four-poster bed.

The house also had the advantage of being near Spring Street School, the public school where Cap would begin his education. And in a pinch the church was within walking distance.

Dr. Broyles had a chance to value proximity to the church the bitter winter of 1942, when Atlanta had a record-breaking ice storm that immobilized transportation and blacked out thousands of homes on Christmas Eve. The church had a tradition of prayer and carols on Christmas morning, and many Atlantans grew up knowing that they could not open their Christmas gifts until after they had been to church to meditate a little on the meaning of Christmas. But Christmas 1942 looked impossible. Phone lines were down, and streets were iced over and slick. The city was silent and white.

Vernon felt that the Christmas service might not be able to take place, but he did not want to be the one to call it off if by some happenstance some worshippers got there. Slipping and sliding over the icy pavements, he made it to the church and found that the organist, Mrs. Emilie Parmalee Spivey, and some of the singers had arrived. The sanctuary was still cold and nearly empty.

Did the musicians want to go on?

Mrs. Spivey looked around at the faces of the singers and the instrumentalists, who were engaged to play at special services. Of course, they wanted to go on, she said. They were in a way show people, and in that tradition they intended the show to go on.

(Later during the ministry of Dr. McFerran Crowe, four of the professional singers, who made up a much-admired quartet for the church, were delivered an ultimatum. They had been moonlighting at a night club downtown. They could give that up or resign from the church choir. They chose the night spot.)

That Christmas Day they were still dedicated to the church's music, and they sang the old Christmas hymns and some of the traditional folk songs like "Little Jesus Boy," which was an annual solo by the contralto, the gifted Alice Tomlinson. Candles were lit against the darkness, and gradually members of the congregation began to arrive. The church was by no means filled, but Vernon looked out on the Christmas-morning faces of enough people of all ages to know that it had been right to go on with the service.

A young soldier was later to confirm that. He had been stopped in Atlanta by the ice storm while on his way to his home in North Carolina for Christmas leave, the last day he would have before being shipped overseas. Trains and buses weren't moving. Planes weren't flying. Taxis and the city's trackless trolley system were out of business. The soldier was stuck in a downtown hotel and filled with frustration and homesickness. He decided to take a walk. It was against the advice of his buddies and the hotel help, but he didn't care. If he slipped and broke his neck it would be better than sitting, waiting, and looking out on icicles.

He made skidding, laborious progress as far as North Avenue and Peachtree, where he was stopped by the sounds of organ, trombones, trumpets, and singing voices, and by the gentle light of candles against stained glass windows.

He mounted the icy gray steps and slipped inside. "And the angel said unto them, 'Fear not, behold, I bring you good tidings of great joy,' " read the minister.

"Hark, the herald angels sing," carolled the choir and the congregation.

Months later Dr. Broyles got a stained, ragged letter from a jungle in New Guinea. The young soldier wanted to say thank you for that Christmas service. It was the last memory he had of home. He had been shipped to the Pacific the next day.

The Broyles family was growing. Betsy, named Elizabeth Ellison for Vernon's sister and called "Boo" by a doting congregation for the beguiling girl child in Margaret Lee Runbeck's story, "Our Miss Boo," was born in September 1943. The church was growing,too. It became necessary to have two Sunday morning services to accommodate the crowd, and a building program was launched to expand the balcony — a favorite place for Bena to sit with her toddlers and for other parents with small children.

"Shall we squirm together?" Bena sometimes invited other mothers with lively youngsters. And Vernon, hearing the apologies of nervous young mothers, would say soothingly, "They worry you but they don't worry

91

me. I'm glad to have them in church."

Work began on a chapel on the north side of the church, a small, exquisite sanctuary that would accommodate one hundred people, could accept the overflow from the big church on Sunday mornings, and would be available for small weddings and christenings.

Dr. Broyles also enjoyed having there "Miss Pauline's children," the hundreds of youngsters he kept the proud and the stylish from snubbing. He was awed and humble before the tiny, gray-haired, partially deaf, partially blind, retired school teacher, who had gathered them up and brought them there.

Wellborn Cody, an elder in the church, was to write of her after her death in 1957 that she "has done what all of us are meant to do, gone from house to house in our challenging neighborhood, gathering to her heart and to our church children who were without a House of God....She has broken down prejudice, persuaded the reluctant, led the unbelieving."

Forty-five years later Vernon was to remember Miss Pauline with love and humor: "Poor lady," he said. "She grew old and lost her hearing and her eyesight and she went to Rich's and bought between seven thousand and eight thousand dollars worth of clothes for her children."

And what did the church do?

"Paid the bill," he said, "and then gave her a retirement party."

He was pleased to remember that some of the parents of these children became regular members of the church, and in time he solemnized weddings and later baptized babies for several of Miss Pauline's little converts.

The war years brought many newcomers to the church, most of them temporary — servicemen and women who enjoyed the U.S.O.- type hospitality in the church parlors with games and puzzles and music and cake and coffee, if not always more substantial viands. Eighty-seven young men and six young women left the church to enter the armed forces, and part of the minister's responsibility was to stay in touch with their families, bolstering their hopes when the young ones were out of touch, rejoicing with them when the war news was promising.

Mindful of the numbers of young people who were aimlessly, restlessly roaming the streets of Atlanta with no place to go, North Avenue posted a church member at the corner to invite in any young fellow or girl in a uniform who might be accepting of church hospitality.

One Sunday afternoon an elder, Will Hammond, vice president of the Georgia Power Company, drew the assignment. A serviceman walked by and Mr. Hammond, smiling warmly, asked him if he would care for a cup of coffee. Misunderstanding the question, the soldier flipped the power company executive a quarter and walked on.

Admiral Richard Truly was an active member of North Avenue and in command of a naval training unit at Georgia Tech. He said one day he would like to bring his boys to church. They would be very welcome, the preacher told him, expecting perhaps half a dozen. More than one hundred young men showed up the next Sunday.

"I'm not sure they came voluntarily," Vernon quipped, "but we were glad to have them and members of the church moved over or moved out to make room for them."

It was the beginning of a close relationship with Georgia Tech and the other colleges and universities nearby. Ministers to the students were sent out from the church, and, as soon as the war was over, clubs were founded to acquaint the young veterans with other people their age and to involve them in church programs. One such group, the Couples Club, attracted primarily young marrieds for Sunday night meetings. For these gatherings, the church kitchens provided only minimal help, according to Elizabeth Flinn in her history, *With Feet of Clay*: "The couples took turns preparing the food, for which the church allotted five dollars. To feed thirty or forty people on so small a fee required some careful planning even in those days. Grits and Vienna sausage were a popular menu."

God beholds thee individually, whoever thou art. He calls thee by thy name....Thou does not love thyself better than he loves thee.

From VSB's scrapbook

Vernon's diaries appear at a glance to be mundane entries recording details of the job—the people he saw in his office, the interminable meetings he went to, the calls he made to the homes of members or to patients in the hospital. When it was a matter of confidential counselling he set down initials only, never revealing the nature of a troubled person's problem. The war was ever on his mind, and he went out almost daily to pray with or just sit beside some member in anguish over the absence of a son or husband in the service. The arrival of a death message from the front seldom got to a family much before he was there to stand by.

Mrs. Roy LeCraw, an active church member whose husband had resigned his post as mayor of Atlanta to fulfill his obligation as a colonel in the army reserves, elicited Vernon's admiration.

After visiting her he wrote, "She is being tested with her husband and three boys in service and two others to care for at home."

He was saddened by the death in Italy of a young man named Bobby Hempstead. "The war is not worth one man like Bobby," he wrote. "His poor mother left alone."

As usual he went immediately to see the mother and later wrote: "What a wonder of strength! Husband and son gone in six months. She is solid as rock. God is truly able."

His days were long and sometimes exasperating. He set down with wry humor the visit of a strange woman who appeared unheralded in his office, monopolized a great deal of time, and then confessed that she had already told her troubles to "everybody in town." He worried over conflicts in the congregation and particularly among members of his staff, where one woman unhappily stirred up strife. Reports of bungling by members who held teaching posts or other duties within the church caused him more concern than those who reported to him realized.

"I'll have to work it out," he wrote in his diary about one problem, "without hurting D——(the offender)."

People who relied on his wisdom and strength thought he had bottomless reserves to share, and it was generally true. But being human, he had self doubts like any man, and inner struggles and occasional lapses into despondency when he feared he was not doing a good enough job leading his flock. Sometimes he had trouble with his sermons and recorded sadly, "My mind is dead on its feet." But he always rallied and sometimes marvelled that the sermon he thought he couldn't write turned out to be one of his better ones. Occasionally he felt that he and most ministers were expected to do more than they had time and understanding to handle, and he questioned his preoccupation with details.

"A day of details minus much satisfaction," he wrote at the end of a long day in September 1944. "Mrs.——— (a member of his staff) continues a bad influence because of her unhappy attitude and it worries me no little. Then there is the sure knowledge that being busy about many things leaves no time for the big thing: To BECOME that God's re-

deeming grace may reach people through me."
He added bleakly, "When I realize how far
[away] I am I wonder sometimes how badly I
want it."

Usually he enjoyed his work and was
genuinely fond of his congregation. Still a
predominantly affluent group with many of
the town's social and financial leaders in the
membership, the congregation worked as-
siduously to implement any plans the minister offered for expanding the reach of the
church. They delighted in Vernon's personal
charm and that of Bena and loved to include
him and his pretty wife in parties, concerts,
and sporting events. The Broyleses had tick-
ets to the theater and access to the town's
more stylish clubs, including the select and
carefully contained Piedmont Driving Club,
where the children could invite friends to
lunch and to swim; the Atlanta Athletic Club;
and the Capital City Club, with its opulent,
old-fashioned facilities downtown for meetings and lunch and dinner and its country
club with golf and tennis. Atlanta intellectu-
als recognized in Vernon an inquiring mind,
a ready wit, and an insatiable thirst for knowledge. They invited him to join the Ten Club,
a limited-membership group of male savants,
who met once a month to read scholarly papers, to review world events, and to talk of

challenging books. His pleasure in the Rotary Club, to which he had belonged in Canton, following in his father's footsteps, resulted in many friendships that were helpful through the years as he pushed through major civic and charitable projects.

He put in long hours, beginning early in the morning with a personal period of Bible reading and prayer. He was a prodigious reader of history and old and new works on theology and managed somehow to cover the daily newspapers. At the end of the day he sometimes read a detective story when he was ready for bed and sleep. He was almost inflexible in devoting the first hours of the day to study of the Bible and prayer, finding new insights in the oft-read chapters of the New and Old Testaments. Once in his diary he advanced the theory that politicians should be required to read all of the "O.T.—three times." It has, he added, "all of history and diplomacy and subterfuge of the whole of history."

So demanding was his job that the times with his family seem to have acquired a special poignancy. He painted the kitchen, but it took several spaced-out, interrupted evenings. He cut the grass, played baseball with his son, Cap, took the family to the fair, and on a rare occasion dressed up and took Bena to the Biltmore Hotel for dinner. It was just the two of them, and he rejoiced in the special food, the music, and her pleasure. "She is a peach," he wrote.

The movie *National Velvet* delighted him as much as it did the children when he took an afternoon off to take them to Loew's Grand.

A walk up to the old Tenth Street shopping center to the hardware store or the barber shop with Cap at his side pleased him as an opportunity to get closer to his son. He was on the board of North Avenue Presbyterian School for Girls, which the church had founded in 1909. He took Bebe (Bena III) to enroll her in the first grade and knew firsthand the pangs of a parent committing his little girl to a new and strange experience. "She was excited," he wrote. "I felt empty. God guide and keep!"

Most evenings, even if he was called out to a meeting or by a distress signal from a church member, he managed time to play with the children before their bedtime and, as often as possible, got in a game of Chinese checkers with his wife.

Sometimes a rush of love and gratitude

for her support, her patience, her humor, and her gaiety, impelled him to write, "Bena, God's blessing."

Once, he wrote, she was "knocked out" by a cold, and he managed to leave his study and keep the baby Betsy for two hours so her mother could rest. Money was often scarce with them, and the most they could manage in the way of help was a part-time maid of all work at seven dollars a week. This was a switch from Bena's native Mississippi, where help was plentiful and fond family nearby.

Vernon delighted in opportunities for walks around the pretty, tree-filled Ansley Park neighborhood with "the entire family, including the dog," after dinner. He took special pleasure in his old Canton friend, Jimmie Smyth, who had moved to Atlanta and was an elder in North Avenue church, meeting him for lunch when their midday schedules permitted, and visiting with him at home in the evenings.

Perhaps influenced by the call for wartime victory gardens or maybe feeling a pull to the earth from his childhood days spent on the family farms in Tennessee, Vernon went home to the little city house with its small yard and planted a garden.

It was October and fall gardening season had mostly passed, so he confined himself to planting some bulbs he and Bena had brought from Canton, sowed a turnip patch, and spread winter grass seed over the front lawn. "Sounds rural," he wrote, "but all was in miniature or in handsful."

The tedium of a day of meetings, sometimes "with fireworks," was relieved one afternoon in the early fall when John Brice, the elder of cutaway coat fame, invited the family to a picnic on a creek that ran through some land he owned.

"Eating on rocks in the middle of creek," Vernon wrote. "Sis (Betsy) wading delightedly, rest of children in, too. Mr. Brice is one of God's noblemen, a man who in practice shows the salvation of a simple faith."

A similar outing at the Covington farm of Elder and Mrs. Sam Carson also made the diary. "The good earth brings forth in abundance," he wrote exuberantly. "Scuppernongs, figs, turnip salad, eggs, fish, corn, peppers, okra, tomatoes, apples, pears, flowers of many kinds, butter, sage, muscadines, chickens, pigs. Grand afternoon."

And then inevitably the line that followed almost all outings, "Back home in time to go to officers and teachers meeting of Sunday school. Discouraging attendance."

"A minister's two chief duties are study and pastoral and visiting," Vernon reflected in his diary. "No man can keep a church going without these. Yet to read my day-by-day activity one would think I didn't know it. A big city church really drains you with no time to refill."

A few days later he was to confess: "All the time my brain whirls with plans and hopes for present and future. There is a surging of unrest, not with being here—I am intensely happy—but with the possibilities, most of which I only sense, and with my inabilities. Maybe God is preparing to move through me. I trust so. Meanwhile, it's like being a sea blown into rising waves by the wind."

Days varied from happy and productive to wearisome and sad. There were weddings and funerals and banquets and church business meetings. He missed his first mid-week prayer meeting to be at the side of the wife and mother of a slain soldier. "It hurts and my rebellion against war grows apace," he wrote.

Dr. Flinn, the venerable founding pastor of North Avenue, was so highly regarded by Atlantans in general that his retirement after forty years brought scores of well-wishers to his Druid Hills home, including the governor and the mayor and admirers from all stations of life. Later the church staged a celebration that Vernon whipped up to show the church's love and appreciation. For weeks he and members of the congregation were busy with plans for a big party. The day of the church supper, he wrote, "was one of the happiest of my life," for he had come to love deeply the gentle, kindly man who was his predecessor.

The months of work and prayer resulted in more than six hundred people filling the church dining room and overflowing to the Sunday school rooms. "The spirit of the crowd was His spirit," he wrote. "Dr. Flinn was superb in response."

Vernon's own speech, on which he had spent hours, was good enough that he, as usual, gave God credit for pulling him through it. "One can't describe the night, the fitting tribute to a great leader and the beginning of a new era," he wrote. "I am grateful for the opportunity to have led in the effort so richly deserved, to tell a man while he lives of affection and appreciation."

With the war on, anxious days inevitably followed, and there seemed to be constant calls to comfort bereaved families and to plan memorial services, which he wanted to make something more than a call for pious acceptance and resignation. He wanted to reassure and hearten, and, as he sat in his study seeking inspiration, the little, tedious problems of his staff nagged at him. One afternoon his friend, Dr. William Gardner, pastor of First Presbyterian Church a dozen blocks up Peachtree Street, dropped in with advice.

Leave off agonizing for a couple of hours, Bill Gardner directed, and let's go to the ballgame. When they got back, Vernon reentered his study, cheered and refreshed, and completed his sermon. "God was present to help," he wrote, and the service was what he had tried to make it. "God is surely good to me with the pressure. He has not left me stranded one time in spite of a mind and heart that are unworthy."

Church membership was growing, expansion of the sanctuary was going to be necessary, and Vernon was naturally pleased. But he cautioned himself not to value numbers too much. However, when Sunday night services, long since abandoned by many churches, showed a dwindling attendance, he redoubled his effort to make them appealing. The formality of morning worship might be appropriate, he decided, and he started wearing his robe at the evening service, too. He brought more music into the service and worked harder on his Sunday-night sermons. There was a small increase in attendance, but eventually the old-fashioned Sunday-night meeting, historically a part of all Protestant churches, had to give way to newer projects, such as the Couples Club, a gathering of young marrieds and some singles for supper and special programs to which visiting theologians and often missionaries were invited to speak.

The church had two holiday services that were very special to its members and to which Vernon brought fresh ardor. One was the Christmas morning hour of carols and meditation and the reading of the Christmas story. The other, perhaps unique to North Avenue, was a Thanksgiving service, dating from 1900 — shortly after the completion of the church. Dr. Flinn began then with the reading of Governor Bradford's 1633 proclamation calling the Plymouth colonists to gather "on ye meeting house on ye hill." They had suffered mighty hardships during their first year in the New World, losing almost half of the colony to death. In the quaint language of the time

*Vernon and
Bena Virden
Broyles in
Canton,
Mississippi,
soon after
their marriage
in 1935.*

*Vernon and Eloise Darby Broyles
after move to Big Canoe in late 70s.*

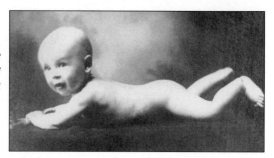

Vernon S. Broyles, Jr., 6 months. Note the magnifying glass – always a stickler for details.

Dr. Broyles' parents: Vernon Seba and Ella Mae Ellison Broyles.

5 years old and on the way to a Mobile fishing hole.

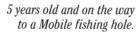

Three generations in early 1940s: Father, son Vernon, Jr., and grandson, Vernon III.

Martha, Vernon's stepmother, his father, Bena, Bena (Bebe), and Vernon III (Cap) in Atlanta – 1940s.

Vernon and youngest daughter, Betsy.

A lot of Broyles – and all first cousins.

Vernon at Davidson College in the roaring 20s.

The Priestly Home, Canton, MS, an antebellum home where Vernon lived until his marriage to Bena Virden.

Out of seminary and on "Dig" at American School of Oriental Research.

First Presbyterian Church, Canton, MS – his first full-time ministry.

North Avenue honors the Broyles family upon his departure in 1950 to become Executive Secretary of the General Assembly's Board of Church Extension.

Dr. Broyles with Dr. Richard Orme Flinn, who preceded him as pastor, North Avenue Presbyterian Church, Atlanta.

An avid reader and student of the Bible.

Vernon looks on in 1948 as Miss Pauline Dennis greets a few of the 1000 children she had brought to the North Avenue Sunday School over a period of nine years.

Celebrating the planting of a new Presbyterian Church.

1960 – Breaking ground for North Avenue's new activities building.

North Avenue hosts "This Is Your Life." Vernon with sister Elizabeth, 1959.

Vernon with Joe Horsley, World Missions Conference chair. Everyone's happy – the Goal was reached!

A great tradition – remembering the pilgrims first Thanksgiving and giving thanks for present blessings, 1971.

Dr. Broyles welcomes Mrs. Flinn and her son William Flinn on the occasion of a reception for retired Presbyterian ministers.

Session members Edward Thomas and James Reaves pay tribute to Dr. and Mrs. Broyles on his retirement from North Avenue Presbyterian Church, 1976.

Dr. Broyles speaks to residents of Presbyterian Village at ceremony to celebrate the lobby named in his honor.

Elders and ministers enjoying a social event. Back row: Fred Lockwood, Dr. Broyles, Dr. Zach Jackson, "Red" Carmichael. Front row: Cook Freeman, Associate Pastor, and Walter Susong.

Dr. Broyles visiting Elizabeth Bloodworth at age 5 months.

Dr. Broyle's congregation at North Avenue Presbyterian Church, 1965. Note children's choirs, which he loved.

North Avenue Church in 1966 entertained the Braves. Dr. Broyles and Mayor Ivan Allen greet two players and a wife.

Dr. Broyles dedicates the Arthur L. Montgomery Building as the new home of Christian Council of Metro Atlanta. Also pictured are Mr. Montgomery and Dr. Harold E. Moore, 1987 President of Council.

Another special community interest, 1967.

Mr. George Woodruff and Dr. Broyles in thoughtful conversation.

Celebrating Founder's Day, Westminster Schools, Dr. Pressly, President of Westminster Schools, Dr. Broyles, Chair, and Mrs. Polly Orr Bates.

Portrait unveiled at dedication of Broyles Arts Center.

Friends gather to greet Dr. Broyles at opening of Vernon S. Broyles Arts Center at Westminster.

A Broyles birthday celebration at Big Canoe. Ann Cousins' comments have Dr. Broyles' attention.

80th Birthday Celebration at Big Canoe – The wonderful touch of friendships. Ed Noble gets a hug while Wayne Smith looks on.

The Broyles joins North Avenue friends at wedding reception.

Arthur Howell presents Dr. Broyles with replica of his portrait which hangs in the Broyles Community Center at Big Canoe.

*The Tom Otsbys and Jimmie Smyth
are pictured with Eloise and Vernon
in their Big Canoe home.*

*Eloise and Vernon enjoying life
at Santorini in 1969.*

*Vacations meant variety. The Mississippi
Queen was another good experience.*

*Vernon enjoys a little playful
relaxation with Paul Duke.*

The Broyles and Darby families gather in late 1980s for special celebration at Big Canoe.

Baby Brian came all the way from Germany for baptism by Dr. Broyles. He was accompanied by grandfather Austin Williams and parents, Delia and Wilhelm Rutzy.

Charlene Terrell walks toward Chapel with Dr. Broyles.

Friends gather after the ground breaking of Broyles Community Center at Big Canoe. Standing with Dr. Broyles is Tom Cousins. Ken Rice, Paul Duke, and others are in background.

Lucretia Davenport, Chapel Trustee, on informal planning mission with Dr. Broyles. He has his 3x5 card in his shirt pocket.

"It's gone far beyond anything I could have dreamed in the beginning. It's a witness that where God is honored, something happens ... the Lord honors those that honor Him."

he called for renewal of hope, for gratitude for the friendship of the Indians, and "ye plentiful harvest" of corn and turnips and potatoes.

Mrs. J. M. High, the wife of a wealthy department store owner, whose Peachtree Street mansion was to become the High Museum of Art and later the nucleus of the present Atlanta Memorial Art Center, had been traveling in Scotland. She brought home from the Queen's "kirk" sprigs of ivy that members took out and planted to climb on and soften the new granite walls. They sang "Amazing Grace" and "Blessed Be the Tie That Binds" as they worked.

Thanksgiving morning at this service set the mood for the holiday observance for most old-time North Avenue members and for many other Atlantans. Vernon carefully preserved its informality. It was held in the sunny Sunday school room where light streamed in through clear windows and an elderly woman named "Miss Nora" Northen thumped out camp-meeting hymns on a piano.

Vernon read the scripture and followed it with the names of members who had died since the last Thanksgiving. He spoke without sadness but with gratitude for the lives they had lived. From time to time, not Presbyterian-like but more like Quakers, members of the congregation would feel moved by the spirit to stand and say what they were thankful for. Dignified elders, schooled in the reticence of the denomination, often led the speaking and women and youngsters followed suit. In the war years gratitude often centered on the safety of some boy on a distant battlefield or sometimes just a letter that was proof that he was alive. After a few spirited, foot-tapping hymns there were hugging and some tears among the departing worshippers.

This was a traditional service that Vernon was glad to keep alive. But when he left the church—that came later—he forgot to explain its unique features to the august Dr. Wallace Alston, a minister and good friend who left his pastorate at Druid Hills Presbyterian to head the prestigious women's college, Agnes Scott, and took a turn at supplying at North Avenue. He was an elegant, eloquent preacher and members were grateful for his brilliant sermons. But on Thanksgiving morning, assembled beneath the stained glass windows of the sanctuary, with the organ and a choir attending, they were homesick for the rousing, almost childlike in their simplicity, Thanksgivings of the past.

They listened to the scripture, they joined in the responsive reading of the Psalter. They were attentive as Dr. Alston spoke of Thanksgiving. They sang the doxology and the Gloria Patri—and they were restless and a little sad on their holiday morning.

It might have ended that way but somebody—nobody now knows who—said something to Dr. Alston. He did a surprising thing. He descended to the floor of the sanctuary and faced the gathering.

"You almost let me do a terrible thing," he said gently. "Through ignorance I was about to change the Thanksgiving service which has been held in the church since 1900."

He picked up the old proclamation and the service was promptly restored. He mentioned that he had found out about their special joyous, un-Presbyterian way of testifying to God's goodness on Thanksgiving Day and now they would please proceed.

They did, some shyly, some in relief and buoyant good humor, thanking God for families and health and plain practical things, for their town and their church. And then from the back of the room a voice called out, "Can't we have 'Old Time Religion,' Dr. Alston?"

Laughing, Dr. Alston appealed to the organist, Mrs. Spivey. "Have you got 'Old Time Religion' up there, Mrs. Spivey?"

She nodded emphatically.

The old camp-meeting hymn poured from the organ. The young people's choir picked it up. The congregation joined in lustily.

The Thanksgiving of Dr. Flinn and Vernon Broyles lived.

*And Jesus increased in wisdom and stat-
ure and in favor of God and man.*
Westminster's motto

Because of his own schooling at University Military School in Mobile and later at
Davidson College and Union Theological
Seminary, Vernon believed strongly in incul-
cating Christian principles in the young as a
major obligation of schools.

Public schools then permitted the Lord's
prayer and a bit of Bible reading,but that was
not enough to provide the basis for teaching
Christian values along with the curriculum.
In 1909 a North Avenue man, who wanted his
son taught the Bible at school, had raised the
question at a meeting of the church session:
Why could not the church organize and conduct such a school?

Dr. Flinn was present and so were several other men who had children of school
age. They agreed. A board of directors was

formed and a school was launched in the Sunday school room with twenty-one third and fourth graders.

By 1910 the church had acquired the McCabe residence next door on Peachtree Street for $20,000, and in 1914 the growing school moved there—with a budget of $14,752. In 1920 the school was incorporated with the stated purpose of "imparting instruction and training in the principles of the Christian religion and in the teachings of the Holy Bible and in addition thereto educational training and instruction in the ordinary and usual grammar and high school branches." A beautiful old residence on Ponce de Leon was acquired in 1921 to accommodate the growing enrollment, and the school flourished—not only for its stated purpose of religious emphasis but also because of its very real insistence on scholarship. Many members of the church sent their children there and like-minded Atlantans followed suit.

Dr. Marion McH. Hull, a North Avenue elder and physician, served as chairman of the school's board of directors from 1919 until his death in 1950. As pastor of the church, Dr. Broyles was automatically a member of the board, and at Dr. Hull's death he succeeded to the chairmanship.

About the same time an honor and an opportunity to work at a higher level and in a wider field in the denomination's hierarchy was offered Dr. Broyles. He had been instrumental in developing a board of church extension to help the struggling churches throughout the southeast and to spearhead building programs for new ones. He was asked to take the job of executive secretary.

Reluctant to leave North Avenue and considering himself "a preaching preacher," he nonetheless felt that the new job was important and that he had no right to turn it down.

It would mean traveling and preaching in dozens of churches in the southeast, being constantly on the road by plane and train, meeting new people in little towns and country places and in some cities where population growth had burgeoned ahead of church building.

Headquarters for the new board would be in Atlanta. He would live at home, but he and his family would transfer their church membership to Morningside Presbyterian. He would retain his positions and memberships in many local institutions, including the chairmanship of the North Avenue Presbyterian School's board.

Things had not been going well with that school since the war ended. Enrollment was down to twenty-one pupils. It seemed inevitable that the school should be closed, but Vernon was probably more reluctant than any of the other trustees to pronounce the death sentence. He loved the school. He sent his own daughters there and was proud that it originated at the church and maintained ties there. He was sentimentally attached to its annual Christmas program, which continued to be held in North Avenue's sanctuary. Through the years the program did not vary much from its theme carol, "Watchman Tell Us of the Night." High school girls sang Handel's "Come Unto Me Weary and I will Give You Rest." Eighth graders in white robes moved down the aisle carrying lighted tapers. Little children sang the songs of the "Friendly Beasts":

I said the donkey all tattered and brown,
I carried his mother to Bethlehem town....
I said the dove from the rafters high
We cooed him to sleep, my mate and I.

There were other carols, and the program ended with "O Holy Night" and then Vernon's benediction. He loved the program and the school, but after the war ended it was clear that North Avenue Presbyterian School, called

"NAPS," was on the way out, too. Enrollment had dropped alarmingly.

Five members of the board met to effect its demise. Vernon wasn't reconciled. He felt that the school could be saved, and he talked to a number of people who might help. One of them was Fritz Orr, who had conducted summer camps for Atlanta youngsters for many years on a beautiful wooded tract of land of several hundred acres north of town near West Paces Ferry Road. He had thought it a good place for a school, and he was definitely interested when the North Avenue trustees talked a bit about moving the school and starting over. If they were interested in his land he would sell at a very reasonable price. Suddenly the meeting of the trustees took a different tack. They wouldn't close the school, they would give it new life in a new location. As chairman of the endeavor, Vernon knew that a dynamic leader would be needed to build and head the new NAPS.

Dr. J. R. McCain, president of Agnes Scott College, undertook the search for a proper educator. As Dr. William L. Pressly wrote in his book, *The Formative Years at Atlanta's Westminster Schools*, he was considering leaving the prestigious McCallie School, founded by his wife's family in Chattanooga, at the time he received a letter from Dr. McCain asking him to suggest the names of three or four headmasters who might be interested in coming to Atlanta to start a school.

The board of trustees, Dr. McCain promised, would give the headmaster virtually free rein in spearheading the development of the new school. "I wrote Dr. McCain," related Dr. Pressly, "that I knew of only one person who might be interested. His name: Bill Pressly."

Dr. Pressly's acceptance of the job gave Vernon a surge of hope for the school. He considered him the best possible choice to head a new school, which they promptly re-christened Westminster because of its Presbyterian connotation. (The Westminster Confession of Faith was accepted by Presbyterian churches in Westminster Abbey in 1649.)

The new school would have a board of trustees comprised of two-thirds Presbyterians and with one Presbyterian minister for every seven board members.

A hundred acres was acquired from Mr. Orr—on credit—and there were fifty additional acres in prospect. "The board of trustees unmistakably made a savvy investment," recalled Dr. Pressley. "For a mere ninety thousand dollars, Westminster owned one hundred acres of what is now some of Atlanta's most expensive real estate."

About that time the trustees learned that Miss Emma Scott, who headed the beautiful Washington Seminary out Peachtree Street, had celebrated her eightieth birthday and was planning to retire. The school had been founded by grandnieces of George Washington in 1878 for fashionable young ladies. It occupied one of the most imposing buildings on Peachtree Street, a mansion boasting twenty-six white zinc Corinthian columns with fluted shafts and capitals of stylized acanthus leaves. The famed *Gone With the Wind* author, Margaret Mitchell, had been "a seminary girl," and she once told an interviewer that, contrary to reports that *GWTW* was her sole work of fiction, she had written some racy short stories while she was in school there. She had sent them off to H.L. Mencken's *Smart Set*, which promptly rejected them.

"I never understood why they didn't buy them," she joked. "The girls at the seminary thought they were grand."

Washington Seminary was to be closed and its site sold for commercial development.

The two schools, Vernon and his fellow trustees decided, should not be closed but
blended. Both the seminary mansion and the
less grand one occupied by NAPS could be
maintained temporarily until the new
Westminster could be built.

Money was needed, and the trustees hired
a New York firm of professional fund raisers
to handle a campaign for a million dollars. A
big campaign convocation and kick-off dinner was planned for the Piedmont Driving
Club's ballroom. A week before it was to be
held, a representative of the fund-raising firm,
in town to survey the situation, wanted to call
the whole thing off. The dinner should be can-
celled, he said. The campaign would fail, and
as for himself and his firm, he was ready to
take a plane back to New York.

Dr. Broyles faced him calmly. "You will
stay," he said. "The dinner will be held. The
campaign will succeed." And that's what happened.

Dr. Pressly was to tell that story many
times through the years. Two decades later
when the school honored Dr. Broyles by un-
veiling a portrait of him in Pressly Hall, Dr.
Pressly related the successive fund drives and
told of the business leaders Dr. Broyles had

selected to head them.

"Many strong men and women have helped secure the millions it has taken in developing Westminster," he said, "but always it has been Dr. Broyles's careful planning that has set the whole thing in motion."

Vernon remained chairman of the Westminster board for an unprecedented twenty years. He had previously served as chairman of NAPS trustees for five years.

On October 15, 1988, the school dedicated a handsome new building to house all its arts, including a five-hundred-seat auditorium with an orchestra pit, eight practice rooms, and a foyer gallery for professional art exhibits. The new building was named the Broyles Art Center.

At the present time, the school that replaced little NAPS and the seminary occupies a 188-acre campus with fourteen buildings and seventeen hundred students. It continues to require courses which, as Vernon hoped, are designed to make students "Biblically literate." Its graduates are admitted to the toughest colleges and universities in the country.

Westminster was the first independent school in the country to be integrated. Atlanta public schools had already integrated in 1961. Atlanta institutions were girding themselves to abolish segregation, and churches, although not in the forefront, were making an effort. North Avenue was in the contradictory position of having no black members but was welcoming African worshipers on a regular basis.

Vernon, who had voted for the integration of Westminster, was amused by the fact that conservatives in the church accepted African blacks with good grace but weren't going to be hospitable to Atlanta blacks. He set about preparing the session to receive black worshippers at North Avenue Presbyterian Church, if and when they came.

Ushers were instructed to greet them at the front door cordially and to conduct them to seats in the sanctuary. If there was any question that the occupant of a pew wouldn't be hospitable, the usher was directed to take his seat with the black visitors, constituting a sort of mannerly buffer.

Only three came and they did not return. Meanwhile members of the Atlanta Christian Council, an organization of ministers that

Vernon had helped to revitalize and find good quarters for, adopted a manifesto urging peaceful desegregation and calling on Christian people to "seek to understand and apply the teachings of our Lord and Master" to the issue. The document listed five principles the ministers advocated: 1. Freedom of speech must be preserved. 2. Christians have an obligation to obey the law. 3. The public school system must not be destroyed. 4. Hatred and scorn for those of another race...can never be justified. 5. Communication between responsible leaders of the races must be maintained. 6. "Our difficulties cannot be solved in our own strength or in human wisdom. It is appropriate therefore that we approach our task in a spirit of humility, penitence and of prayer."

Eighty ministers from all denominations signed the manifesto, which made the front pages of the Atlanta papers, the *New York Times*, and many other newspapers. Vernon was not one of the signers. When asked about it years later he was surprised. He concurred with the statement wholly, he said, and a year later when a similar resolution was passed by the council, he did sign it.

The beautiful Jewish Temple on Peachtree Street was dynamited in October

1958, causing the *Atlanta Constitution* editor-publisher Ralph McGill in a prize-winning editorial to call it the "harvest of Christian ministers who have chosen to preach hate instead of compassion." It was a generality that didn't apply to the ministers Vernon knew, but he thought it was a point not to be lightly dismissed. The following Sunday he quoted in his sermon the words of the Greek author Aeschylus that were later to serve as the epitaph for Robert Kennedy: "To tame savageness of man and make gentle the life of the world."

When Martin Luther King, Jr., was assassinated in 1968, North Avenue was one of the many Atlanta churches that opened their doors to the thousands of mourners who came into town for the funeral and followed the body of the civil rights leader on its mule-drawn cart in what his widow called "his last great march." The church kitchen was kept open and cots were set up in the Sunday school rooms for those who might need them.

7

Life caved in!
VSB's journals

In the midst of the victorious campaign for Westminster Schools and many sustaining, satisfying friendships, including one with the man who was soon to be mayor of Atlanta, Ivan Allen, Jr., trouble hit Vernon Broyles and his family.

His diary said it simply: "Tuesday, Feb. 3, at noon life caved in! Bena apparently has cancer of the breast. Drs. Denton and Scarborough are worried about its rapid development. It has eclipsed nearly everything in my mind and heart. She is to be operated on Monday. She is a wonder and is apparently not frightened. I confess I am and there is a raging struggle for faith in my heart that brings peace and assurance. My faith is fixed. That is not the question. Getting it to relax my stomach is the crucial point. Already I have discovered God promises nothing but Himself, which is peace, and this is gain. The valley is still not well lighted but there is a Presence and I'm moving forward. It is going to be hard until we know Monday. We are truly in the hands of God—beyond any arranging I can do. God have mercy on us all and give thy healing if it can possibly be found in thy will. Fix my faith on 'one day at a time' and on the sufficiency of the today."

There were no entries in his diary for two weeks and then: "Life has changed. Doctors discovered a malignant breast of Bena's. One week ago it was removed.

"The two weeks have been desolate with a constant fight against fear. The question 'WHY?' is not too much the point and I thank God for this. Fear of her suffering, fear of the future for the children clamor at the heart."

In the months that followed he picked up his travels and his meetings with churches all over the South, but his mind was on Bena and the children, and his pleasure in riding along in the countryside and seeing flowers and birds was no more.

Along the gulf coast he saw an old couple tottering along in the sand. He may have realized that no halcyon old age awaited him and Bena, and he was seized by sudden heartbreak.

Pelicans were diving beyond the surf and he identified with them. "Like a pelican diving for fish," he wrote, "I seem to be suspended always, ready to dive—and diving. There is little enjoyment in moments or days when all goes well. Guilt plays a part. Maybe I can't accept myself or am afraid others (God) can't or won't."

He feared the loss of faith and of security. He wrote: "Bena and the children are the finest in the world. God care for them." He felt that he was preaching the gospel "hesitantly" and promised to do better.

Bena's operation appeared to be satisfactory, but he worried. "There is the matter of recurrence with which we must live. People everywhere are praying. I can feel it. My prayer is that she shall be given a reasonable period without further trouble—some ninety years. God through Christ can carry her to health and keep her there. If ever a servant of His deserved God's healing and mercy by her faith in Christ and surrender she does. But one hesitates to talk of 'deserts.' "

At his busiest times, working for Westminster Schools, conferring with civic and philanthropic leaders, Vernon fought fear, and when he was alone with his diary he conscientiously expressed gratitude for friends but added, "Fear is hard to check. Confidence is hard to bring to birth." He realized that he was experiencing what he had been preaching about to others. He affirmed to himself what he well knew, that surrender was the key.

"Real surrender is not easy and perfect trust waits on the surrender. Fear is selfish mainly and this is in a sense humiliating. I thank God that he has not left me in these days. Surely the past is eloquent of His love."

Bena was undergoing treatment at Emory University Hospital when an almost unprecedented thing for a minister happened to Vernon. He got a call to return to his beloved North Avenue church.

No minister that any of them knew had been given a call back to a church he had left. It would be like going home, picking up something he had started, being surrounded in his family's greatest travail by old, tried and true friends. He would no longer be a "traveling man" but would be able to be within a dozen blocks of Bena and the children throughout most days. But as much as he wanted it he had to be sure it was not his selfishness but God's will.

"Vernon prayed over it," Bena reported joyfully, "and I packed!" It was a figure of speech because they had not moved out of their house during his years with church extension.

Mac Crowe had not entirely suited North Avenue, and he seemed to know it. In one of his final sermons he said that he had never "wholly won the hearts of the congregation." Their hearts belonged to Vernon Broyles. And his heart belonged to them.

In July 1954 the Broyleses returned to North Avenue to a tumultuous welcome. Dr. Crowe re-inducted him, saying that Vernon had never really left and that now he was officially "back where he belongs."

When Vernon gave up the job of overseeing and guiding hundreds of Presbyterian churches throughout the South and returned to the one he counted his own, the turmoil in his heart and mind was almost matched by the turmoil of the city and state. He kept his anxiety and uncertainties to himself so the church at large was unaware of his suffering. A few friends knew but Bena, perky and smiling and smartly dressed as always, was still on her feet and moving through all the church activities.

She attended the annual luncheon of her Sunday school class, named for its founding teacher, Dorothy (Mrs. Whitner) Howard, and the one she went to when she wasn't needed to play the Sunday school piano. Someone who had just read James Street's novel about the temptations and infidelities of ministers, jokingly asked her if it gave her concern.

She smiled. "I don't think the temptations are any greater for preachers than they are for doctors and lawyers or any other man," she said. Her face alight with a gamin smile, she added mischievously, "I'm sure half the women in the church are in love with Vernon—and that's fine." Everybody laughed because they knew that Bena's hold on her husband's affections was secure.

Even their children weren't totally aware of the almost certain tragedy awaiting them. Their parents told them of Bena's illness but so calmly that devastating grief and fear did not encompass them. Vernon knew the whole truth, and his daily sessions of prayer became fervent pleas for strength and acceptance.

Years later, going through his library, friends found tucked in a book a prayer Vernon had written revealing naked depths of anguish and despair. He asked forgiveness for sins nobody could believe were his: unbelief, fear, sensuousness, ingratitude, hypocrisy, selfishness, pride, unrest, lovelessness. "Make me kind in word and deed," he pleaded, "honest, patient, uncritical, grateful to God and to people." And then piteously, urgently, "Take care of our children. Give me grace to surrender Bena, the children, myself to the future—to God of Jesus Christ."

Meanwhile, the quiet mind he asked for was not available to most of the country. Civil rights demonstrations broke out around the country, and Atlanta, preparing to celebrate "M" Day, the day when its population would reach a million, was not immune. The longtime mayor, William B. Hartsfield, and the police chief, Herbert Jenkins, were determined to keep the peace, as were most Atlantans. But the governor, south Georgian Marvin Griffin, was pledged to resist all efforts to integrate the public schools and colleges of the state.

One of his thrusts brought demonstrations almost to the doorstep of his neighbors on The Prado, the Broyleses. At that time the Governor's Mansion was an old Stone Mountain granite residence in Ansley Park just a few blocks from the Broyleses' small white clapboard house. The governor demanded that the board of regents prohibit the Georgia Tech football team from playing a Sugar Bowl engagement with the University of Pittsburgh because Pittsburgh had a black player on its team. Outraged Tech students marched on the Governor's Mansion and hanged the chief executive in effigy. The game went on. But the Ku Klux Klan, which had been quiescent for many years, surfaced again and demanded a police escort for a downtown motorcade. It was refused, and the Grand Dragon mounted a soap box to declaim against the city of Atlanta. "We ought to get our capital moved out of that buzzard roost!" he cried.

Many white people were moving to the suburbs, taking their church memberships with them to newer churches, which were going up on the northside. Most North Avenue members were faithful to their old church, but it was getting too small. The sanctuary accommodated only 550 people, and even with a second, earlier Sunday morning service at 8:30 A.M., it was so crowded that the ushers had trouble seating all comers. Charles Swanson, an elder reporting on the problem, said that Cliff Carson, who was in charge of the ushers, packed worshippers so tightly that they called him "the sardine king." If you stood up to sing, Mr. Swanson recalled, you might find your seat in the pew taken when you started to sit down. The old church also needed serious repairs. It had a leaky roof, and although there was no bell and there were no bats in the belfry, there was a flock of roosting pigeons. They had no regard for keeping sabbath peace.

Mr. Swanson remembered: "I'll never forget one Sunday Dr. Broyles came to a very dramatic moment in his sermon and intoned solemnly, 'And a voice from heaven...'. Suddenly a pigeon cooed loudly. It was one of the few times I ever saw Dr. Broyles speechless."

North Avenue was the first church in Atlanta to have air conditioning, a primitive system involving a fan blowing over blocks of ice, but it worked very well except when there were standing-room-only crowds at the church and the doors had to be left open.

Expansion and rebuilding were indicated. A massive construction program was launched. The congregation borrowed quarters again, not from Methodists this time but from a Jewish theatrical entrepreneur named Sam Rothberg, who owned the legitimate Erlanger Theatre just beyond the vacant lot where the old McCabe residence had been next door. While the walls of the church were being pushed back and new foundations laid, services were held where a short time before Tallulah Bankhead and other show-business stars from Broadway had played.

Vernon had a policy against nagging the congregation for money but the elders did not. They launched a campaign that netted $450,000. Everybody helped. Even the young-sters had their money-raising project—a car wash in the parking lot back of the church.

Wellborn Cody, a prominent Atlanta at-torney and a member of the session, served as finance chairman, going forth to deal with banks. He got a three-year mortgage and re-turned to find that mortgaging their church was an abomination to some members. Mr. Cody went back to the bank and got a remark-able deal—a five-year loan without collateral and promise of an extension if it became nec-essary.

Bena was undergoing X-ray therapy at Emory University Hospital and was ill on many days but remained mobile and contin-ued to be active in the church. She watched the progress of the building program with in-terest. To a diehard member who complained that it wouldn't be the "same" church with-out the dark red carpets and the heavy curved pews, she said firmly, "It's going to be beautiful! Light and space ... lovely!"

For almost three years after Dr. Elliott Scarborough, head of the celebrated Winship Cancer Clinic at Emory, with Dr. Henry Finch, a physician elder at North Avenue to assist him, knew that the spread of the cancer was irrevocable, Bena kept going. "She had great spirit," said Dr. Finch. "She would stay on her feet and move."

But the summer of 1956 was hot and debilitating, and finally she took to her bed. Some members of the church, who wanted the gift to remain anonymous, added a downstairs bedroom and bath to the house and installed air-conditioning, which was not yet common in residences. "Vernon was very grateful for that," Dr. Finch said. "Bena herself held out a few months longer than we had expected."

Betsy Primm, a friend of Betsy Broyles since the seventh grade, remembers it as the year when all the little girls in their class had Coke parties after school — "so sophisticated." Betsy Broyles could seldom attend, she recalled, because her mother was ill and she might be needed at home. And of course they didn't expect her to give a party. But she did. On Valentine's Day she invited her friends to a fine spread of Cokes and cookies and little sandwiches artfully cut into heart shapes.

"Her father did it," said Betsy Primm. "Dr. Broyles passed the refreshments and welcomed us all. It was the first time we had seen a father do that. I think we might have been a little uncomfortable and I'm sure he was."

Bena was not strong enough to see the light-and-space filled sanctuary finished. She was conscious and able to have visitors until the last few weeks, and she was as delighted as Vernon with the news that their old friend from Canton, Jimmie Smyth, who had followed them to Atlanta a couple of years after they had arrived, had found someone he wanted to marry. Vernon had met the bride-to-be, Virginia McIntire of Ardmore, Oklahoma, and had promised them that he would be out there on their wedding day to perform the ceremony. The date was set for December 3, but a few days before the wedding Vernon called the couple with the news that Bena's condition was worse and he could not come. She died on December 2.

"She had been in the hospital for a while," Betsy recalled. "I know now that everyone knew she was dying and I should have known. I was plenty old enough (thirteen years old) to understand that but I didn't. Her brother, Wilson Virden,had come to Atlanta to see her. It was Sunday. Late in the afternoon Bena [Bebe] and I went out to the hospital to see her. As I recall Daddy was going to take Wilson to the airport.

"I still remember walking into the room. There were several people around her—doctors and nurses, I guess. She looked up at us and smiled and raised her hand in a gentle wave but I don't think she could talk. But she knew we were there."

Betsy doesn't remember clearly but she thinks her sister was probably told to call their father and tell him that "Mother was slipping." Vernon arrived and was in the room with Bena when death came.

"After she died," Betsy went on, "we all sat together a while in a small lounge there at the hospital. I remember Cap calling while we were still there and Daddy telling him Mother was already gone."

As they were leaving, someone in the elevator told them that that afternoon they had heard Bena say "a quiet prayer for Jesus to take her."

Cap, a student at his father's Davidson College, alma mater of so many Presbyterian ministers, had not known that his mother's condition had deteriorated. He had not come home. An assistant dean found him and told him his mother was "gravely ill, near death." The school promptly arranged a flight home for him, and he finally got his father on the phone from the Charlotte, North Carolina, airport.

"He said—all he said was 'She's gone,' " young Vernon remembered.

Church members rallied around with all the things that family and friends do with food and flowers and hand-holding visits to ease the pain of a suffering man and his children. With the throngs of people who cared about them they knew well what Emily Dickinson called the bustle that death makes in a house. Announcement of Bena's death had been made that night at the Sunday night service at the church, and when Vernon and his children got home they found friends already there.

Betsy recalled, "I can still see them standing by the driveway as we drove up. Daddy put a rollaway bed in his room so I was not alone. I really think all four of us spent the night in the same room but I'm not clear about Be and Cap."

Mechanically they went through the days before and after the funeral, which was conducted by Vernon's associate pastor, Dr. Cecil Lawrence. Vernon's sister, Elizabeth, and her son, Geron, arrived and "helped us get through the days," Betsy said. Her school friend, Betsy Primm, skipped classes and stayed with her.

"I think my overwhelming emotion was one of disbelief," the young woman said, thinking back. "I truly hadn't understood that she was dying. I think I actually handled the grief fairly well at the time because it simply was not 'real.' "

A year later another young associate pastor, Cook Freeman, arrived at North Avenue, but Vernon wasn't there to greet him. "He told me ahead of time he wouldn't be," Mr. Freeman recalled. "It was the anniversary of Bena's death and he had to get away by himself for a bit. I don't know where he went."

The children did not know where he had gone either, but in the interim between a "very hard Christmas with everybody trying too much to make it bearable for everybody else," and time for their schools to reopen, Vernon took the children on what for them was a restorative outing, even if it did little for his spirits. His uncle, Newell Ellison, a Washington lawyer, and his wife, Anne, invited them to visit Williamsburg, which they had never seen.

"We loved it," Bebe remembers. "We also went to a horse race and placed a bet and went around to the paddock to look at the horses. Daddy didn't bet but he always loved horses and he enjoyed looking at those. He was really ground down but he tried to make the trip a pleasure for us. And it certainly was very different for us. We hadn't taken many trips."

Before their holiday Vernon complied with his lifelong conviction that the duties and obligations of a day must be handled that day. A week after Bena's death he was back in the pulpit, and he preached one of the most memorable sermons of his career. The church was to reprint it and distribute it widely to people in time of bereavement. It was called "Comfort in Sorrow," and in Vernon's fashion it took up the dilemma of grief in a simple one-two-three way.

"The first thing," he said, "is that sorrow

is not an alien intruder. Sorrow is at home in the heart of God. He spared not his own Son but delivered him up for us all....God was in Christ standing at the open grave and crying for his friend out of grief. God was in Christ reconciling the world unto Himself as he agonized in Gethsemane, saying, 'My soul is sorrowful unto death!' Hanging there finally on the cross, crying out as almost every human heart sooner or later will cry out or has cried out, 'My God, why has thou forsaken me?' " Grief and sorrow, he continued, are "a part of life as it must be lived" and "one of the ties that bind mankind together."

"The second thing about sorrow," he went on, "is that you and I choose it for ourselves. We choose it because the coin of love has two sides—a side of joy and a side of sorrow. The day you commit yourself to love somebody, the day you accept the love of someone, that day you choose to walk in the valley of the shadow of sorrow, because joy is just one side of the coin of love, and, if you love, one day you are going to lose that which you love....If you are to escape sorrow you must refuse love."

The third thing, he said, is that "sorrow is one of our most precious possessions...because it is in the Garden of Sorrow that we remember those we love...in sadness and yet with a sadness that opens the very gates of Heaven, ...that interprets the meaning of love."

"Comfort comes," he said, "as a part of the mercy and grace of God through surrender"—the surrender of the loved one to God "with the consciousness and conviction that God will do far more than we can ask or think" and the surrender of oneself—"just laying yourself in the arms of God."

"There is not a thing you can do for yourself other than that....It is not easy. It is very like taking a live rubber ball and throwing it up and asking it to stick to the wall. You keep throwing and it keeps bounding back. But it is not exactly like a rubber ball for one day it will stick—this matter of surrender. For a while it will be very difficult."

He paused and his personal admission touched the hearts of his hearers. "Well, all the time it is difficult," he said. "We are human beings and we never perfectly exercise our faith. Do not let it worry you if you surrender and then all of a sudden you have it on your shoulders again and in your heart. Just surrender it and keep surrendering. You will find that even in the imperfection of your surrender there begins to move His Presence."

142

Help comes, he went on, from facing frankly questions and doubts. "Nobody can ever be absolutely sure," he said. "It would not be faith to be absolutely sure. It would be knowledge then. Faith is a jumping out in the dark and finding you do not fall but have about you the everlasting arms....The question that is almost always in the heart is, 'Why did this have to happen to me?' It may sound a little blunt but the best answer insofar as I know is a simple question, 'Why should it not happen to you? Why should it not happen to me?' It happened to the Son of God Himself. It happens sooner or later to everybody else in the world. Why should it not happen to you and me?...It will help you, I think, if you put yourself back down in the caravan of common man and just accept life as it is. Find your place in the sufferings of men. You have company there, the company of all mankind."

He spoke of the ministry of friends and of the future. "It does not help very much to live in the future, particularly where grief and sorrow have come because as you project the future all you can think of is darkness....Therefore we are invited by God to live one day at a time....Every day God does something to light the darkness and if you try to project the future in the midst of your grief you leave all that out. You just plod through darkness. But if you live a day at a time in faith that God will open the way, you will find that every day brings some marvel of His grace...just a day at the time, letting God take the future."

He spoke of the effort of physicians and concerned friends to ease the pain of bereavement with tranquilizers and other drugs. Allowing that there are times for their use, he said, "I want to say to you that these things are robbing men and women of some of their highest experiences. God meant us to live. He did not mean us to run."

And then one of his favorite prescriptions: "It is always important to do the thing that needs doing today. So many people sit back and say, 'Well, I just cannot face it—I cannot do it.' To evade the day's responsibility weakens you for tomorrow. It is always a helpful thing to get going in the ordinary pattern of daily living as soon as possible."

Surrendering, believing, picking up the thread of your life—these three will lead to comfort, he promised. In his final prayer he pleaded: "Leave us not, neither forsake us. Grant that we shall not forsake Thee but, going forth from this place, shall live more generously, more kindly, more lovingly, shall be

144

more perfectly the representatives of that which we profess."

Education and money without a noble cause can only produce tragedy on a grander scale. ...Without God, we will misuse these tools of life in an effort to serve ourselves.
VSB—in church bulletin

In March of 1985 Robert W. Woodruff, the genius behind the Coca-Cola Company for more than half a century, died. He was one of the world's greatest philanthropists, having given away an estimated $350 million to benefit education, medicine, social services, and the arts. Vernon Broyles preached his funeral, joining in the pulpit Dr. Paul Echel, pastor of the church.

It was not Vernon's church. He had simply supplied at First Presbyterian during the months when it was without a pastor, and in any case the philanthropist, not a church-going man, was not a member of the congregation. But years before he had made Vernon promise to "see me off." It connoted a friendship that began in the busy years following

Vernon's return to North Avenue and Bena's death, when he immersed himself in scores of civic and charitable enterprises — and especially in the development of Westminister Schools, whose board of trustees he headed. The relationship soon involved Vernon's real calling, concern for the wealthy magnate's relationship to God.

Vernon couldn't remember why he first called upon Mr. Woodruff. An appointment with the legendary tycoon was not easily come by. Mrs. Lucille Huffman, who had been his secretary for many years, once told an interviewer that Mr. Woodruff "avoids dreary characters like the plague" and "never gets caught with the tedious ones twice." But she knew Vernon was neither dreary nor tedious. He had preached the funeral of a member of her family and had become a friend. When he said he would like to see Mr. Woodruff she arranged it.

Whatever the purpose of his call, Vernon soon forgot it in his concern for Robert Woodruff's spiritual life. "He was a lonely man," Vernon said later. "Everybody who drew near to him was interested in his money. I sat in his office and thought about that, and I made up my mind that I wasn't going to ask him for anything. He was thinking about his faith in God and he wanted to talk about it. I went to see him many times after that and the subject of money never came up."

The friendship grew, and one day Mr. Woodruff told Vernon he would like to join North Avenue church. "I told him that the church would welcome him but I thought he would do better to join First Presbyterian where his family had long been members. He laughed and said, 'All right but you're my pastor and when I die I want you to see me off.' "

Remembering, Vernon grinned. "I told him I'd preach his funeral but he'd better hurry. I was getting old myself."

Early in the century Mr. Woodruff had another personal chaplain, a schoolmate named Richard Gresham with whom he had graduated from Georgia Military Academy (now Woodward Academy) in 1908. Mr. Gresham was pastor of the First Baptist Church of Moultrie, close enough to Mr. Woodruff's Ichuaway Plantation to become a frequent visitor and to participate in hunting and fishing, but not in card games with the Coca-Cola magnate. Friends referred to them, wrote Charles Elliott in his book, *Mr. Anonymous*, as "the reverend and the reprobate." The minister retired and then died.

Mr. Woodruff lived to be ninety-five years old, and the day of his funeral First Presbyterian Church, next door to the mammoth Woodruff Arts Center, which he had endowed, was jammed with dignitaries from all over the nation. Mr. Woodruff had been a friend of presidents, had swapped cigars with Winston Churchill, had hunted and golfed with cabinet members and generals, and even had a favorite pointer on his south Georgia plantation named Dwight Eisenhower for a former frequent house guest.

Many eulogies were to be offered, many affectionate stories were exchanged before and after the funeral.

Ivan Allen, Jr., who had been mayor of Atlanta during the tense days of integration, told how "Mister Bob" had called him the day Atlanta braced itself for the funeral of the slain civil rights leader, Dr. Martin Luther King, Jr. Mr. Woodruff said, "Ivan, the minute they bring King's body back ... Atlanta, Georgia, is going to be the center of the universe. I want you to do whatever is right and necessary, and whatever the city can't pay for will be taken care of. Do you understand what I am saying?"

Only Robert Woodruff would give a city

the size of Atlanta a blank check, the former mayor said. Fortunately the mayor did not have to draw on it.

Vernon began his eulogy with a charming little story. A small black country church had burned to the ground and Mr. Woodruff, hearing about it (probably from Vernon), sent anonymous funds to rebuild it. The congregation eventually learned the identity of the donor and they wrote a note to the Coca-Cola Company which said: "Dear God, thank you for Mr. Woodruff."

Vernon spoke of Mr. Woodruff's gifts to universities, medical centers, the art museum, and to parks. He said, "Behind his life was the consciousness of God's word in Mr. Woodruff's favorite passage of scripture: 'Give and it shall be given unto you; good measure, pressed down, shaken together, and running over shall men give unto your bosom. For with the same measure that you mete withal, it shall be measured to you again.' He continued, 'To whosoever much is given from him shall much be required and it is required of stewards that a man be found faithful.' "

"We are grateful for the interlocking cords that bind us together and we are grateful for every life he touched," Vernon said later at the graveside in Westview cemetery.

Different cords from those that bound Vernon to Mr. Woodruff bound him to Mr. Woodruff's brother, George Woodruff, who was a member of First Presbyterian Church. "Mister Bob," for all his interest in religion, did not take up church attendance. His brother, George, did, and Vernon grew close to him during the months when he alternated with Dr. Alston in the First Presbyterian pulpit, following the illness and departure of the Broyleses' longtime friend, Dr. Gardner.

So devoted a church member was George that the congregation wanted to elect him elder. He told Dr. Broyles about it, and in the midst of the minister's congratulations the younger, eighty-five-year-old Woodruff said that he wanted to ask his brother Bob before he accepted.

Later Mr. Woodruff reported to Dr. Broyles that Bob had said "no." Vernon sympathized with the disappointment that George must have felt. The post of elder in the Presbyterian church is a highly respected office traditionally reserved for esteemed—and in the past—wise and venerable senior members. (In recent years younger men and many women, including Dr. Broyles's two daughters, have ascended to the post in their respective churches.) Even as he sympathized, Vernon was awed by the deep relationship that made George Woodruff feel the need to first talk with his brother before accepting the church office. After all, George was in his own right a wealthy businessman and a philanthropist of great stature. He and his wife gave millions to education, to the family's favorite Emory University, to Agnes Scott College, to Georgia Tech, and to Westminster Schools, among others. Dr. Broyles was also to preach George Woodruff's funeral when he died at the age of ninety-two.

Ivan Allen, Jr., who served as mayor, and his wife, the former Louise Richardson, came to value Vernon as a friend and spiritual adviser during his months at their church.Later the mayor said Vernon was with him during some of the most agonizing decisions he had to make — when public accommodations were integrated and there were demonstrations on both sides, civil rights activists staging sit-ins on the one hand, and racists threatening violence on the other.

"He didn't tell me what to do," the mayor said. "He just stood by. We were close friends with love and respect beyond the church."

Vernon had baptized their third son, Beaumont, and when Mrs. Allen's mother, Mrs. Josephine Inman Richardson, quite an individualist and in her nineties, came to die, she had already decreed that her funeral be held at home and that Vernon Broyles officiate.

It was enough to get Vernon a reputation as "minister to the moneyed," but it wasn't a fair picture. He had involved the church all along in many projects specifically tailored to help the poor and the disadvantaged.

When Cuban refugees poured into Atlanta, North Avenue welcomed them, finding homes, serving up hot meals, conducting English language classes and acting as an employment service. Vernon went to Brazil on a mission for the Presbyterian church in 1965 and met a missionary whose work among poor people touched him very deeply. Five years later when the minister and his family returned to this country, he persuaded them to join him at North Avenue and launch a program that ultimately led to the vastly successful worldwide Friendship Force. The missionary was the Reverend Wayne Smith, who with his wife, Carolyn, and four children, labored in Taguatinga near the new capital of Brasilia.

"He came to the mission field, he saw the work that our denomination was doing there through its missionaries and he conquered my heart," Mr. Smith later wrote the North Avenue congregation. "This man's love and compassion for people was clearly demonstrated as I took him from place to place. Whether he was talking with a humble worker in the person's hovel or conversing with a member of the Brazilian National Congress he treated them all the same. He dealt with them with love....If I had been showing Jesus Christ around Brasilia this is the way the Lord would have acted too."

When Dr. Broyles learned that the Smiths were back in this country he promptly recruited Wayne Smith to become an associate pastor of North Avenue with the special assignment of minister to the community.

The community nearest to the church badly needed help. The Tenth Street area, once filled with pleasant old homes and a popular shopping area of stores and restaurants and a theater, had deteriorated with the arrival of hippies, accompanied by motorcycle gangs and drug dealers.

Early morning sunshine often revealed freshly dressed and coifed old ladies headed for the market with their shopping carts and having to pick their way through sodden, drug-numbed young bodies sprawled across the sidewalk. Crime had increased, some stores closed, the neighborhood school was no more. The movie house pulled down its marquee and quit the neighborhood. The Salvation Army, true to its mission to the lowliest of hungry, homeless, and prison-bent people, moved in, but it was having a tough time.

Determined to save the young girls who were runaways and falling prey to drug dealers and pimps, the Salvation Army opened a lodge especially for girls. The first one was in the heart of the newly dangerous district, so they moved a few blocks away into a still quiet and respectable neighborhood where, they thought, the young women could live and receive help without attracting attention. It didn't work. The neighbors were not deceived. They complained, invoking a zoning law that prohibited such a lodge on their street.

It was a job for Vernon's new associate, Wayne Smith. Oddly enough, North Avenue soon became the lessee of a wonderful 1892 Peachtree Street mansion, once stylish but now half-hidden by modern extensions and improvements and mercifully big enough for a whole roster of agencies. Wayne Smith and Captain Judy Moore, the Salvation Army's director of the lodge for girls, were dazzled by its possibilities but temporarily daunted by its price of three hundred thousand dollars.

North Avenue's Tom Cousins came to the rescue. His sole request was for anonymity, which lasted only temporarily. The young real estate developer said staunchly, "Buy it. I will lease it back to the church for a dollar a year and if it is ever sold I will contribute the profit to any Christian organization you might indicate."

The complex, including a new office building erected to house Red Cross offices in front of the old mansion, became known as "Metanoia," a Greek word meaning "turning around" or a change of direction. It housed not only the imperiled young girls but a galaxy of agencies including the Christian Council of Metro Atlanta; civil liberties groups, including those defending conscientious objectors; a program of assistance to prisoners and their families; and a psychiatric counselling service with crisis intervention for families. There was even a small coffee shop manned by volunteers, where street people and businessmen and businesswomen from the neighborhood often met on a friendly basis. The coffee shop, called the Common Cup, had programs of music and speakers who held community issues forums. In that neighborhood the issues sometimes involved such topics as exorcism and satanism. In the basement there was also an art school with fourteen volunteer professional teachers on its roster.

Metanoia was non-denominational, although North Avenue Presbyterian, its ministers, and one of its members, were the major sponsors. Baptists and Catholics and several other church groups labored there. Until it outgrew its quarters and expanded its services, the Christian Council of Metro Atlanta maintained its headquarters there.

A strong supporter of the Christian Council of Metro Atlanta and its services, Vernon went to a North Avenue member, Arthur Montgomery, and asked that he take on the job of rejuvenating the council, which had fallen on hard times. There was almost no money and nowhere to go since their lease in the old Metanoia facility had expired. Montgomery agreed to accept the challenge and spent the next seven years at the task. He became chairman of the board and expanded it, adding many new and influential members. Also, he undertook a fund-raising campaign, which during that period brought in over four million dollars for the work of the council. A building was purchased, and in gratitude the board named it the Arthur L. Montgomery Building.

For his unflagging interest and support, the council later awarded Vernon one of its rare awards for service. (Only three awards of this caliber have been given in the history of the council.)

Earlier the council had founded and supported mental health homes for patients newly released from the state hospital. After the state assumed support of these places, the council took on other projects of special interest to Vernon, notably a refugee resettlement program similar to the one the church already operated for Cuban immigrants. Three shelters for the homeless, one for women and children, one for men and their families, and a third that offers homeless men a bed and a meal in the wintertime, get much of their support from the council.

Vernon's young associate, Wayne Smith, was soon to go international, and Vernon and the church enthusiastically urged him on.

With the encouragement of Dr. Broyles, Wayne Smith persuaded Jimmy Carter, the newly elected governor, and Mrs. Carter to take a look at the work being done in Brazil and to utilize his services as guide and interpreter.

As a result of that trip, the now-famous Friendship Force, which has resulted in exchange visits between millions of Americans and citizens in most of the other countries of the world, was formed. Two hundred Georgians, many of them members of North Avenue Presbyterian Church, went to Brazil for ten days, staying in the homes of the local people, and a like number of Brazilians soon returned the visit. After Carter became president, he endorsed the formation of the Friendship Force, which put a million more people in touch "across the barriers which divide people," Wayne Smith said. By 1992 there were 364 "friendship" clubs spread through sixty-two countries and all fifty states.

"Without Vernon Broyles's encouragement and backing it wouldn't have happened," Mr. Smith said. "I'll never forget that it started in the basement of North Avenue Presbyterian Church."

North Avenue had its own World Mission Conference, holding an annual week-long campaign to support foreign missions at first, now local missions as well. During this time a North Avenue elder, former mayor Roy LeCraw, and his wife gave of their personal funds and construction materials to build more than a hundred churches in Asia. One of these new churches replaced a tent chapel in which Mr. LeCraw had worshipped as an American officer fighting near Seoul.

Into our lives in many simple, familiar, homely ways, God infuses this element of joy from the surprises of life, which unexpectedly brightens our days and fills our eyes with light.

from VSB scrapbook.

In 1966, ten years after Bena's death, Vernon married again. It was an event his family and friends had been hoping for. His children had grown up and were married.

While on a trip to Russia, Cap had met a Vassar student named Susan B. Anthony for her great, great, great aunt, the famed temperance and woman's suffrage fighter. He still had ahead of him another year at Union Theological Seminary when they were married in 1961. Cap's father and sisters went to Albany, New York, to participate in his marriage to Susan.

Bebe, wearing her mother's wedding dress, was married to her college sweetheart,

George Cates, at North Avenue church with her father and the Cates's minister, the Reverend Allison Williams, officiating.

Betsy was married to Tommy Grimes, a fellow student at Emory, and had moved to his hometown of Jacksonville, Florida. Vernon and Cap shared the honor of solemnizing this ceremony. Vernon walked down the aisle with Betsy, who was wearing the gown of her friend, Linda Dodd, Coach Bobby Dodd's daughter. After he had responded to his minister son's question, "Who giveth this woman?", he placed Betsy's hand in that of the bridegroom, turned and faced the young couple, and finished the ceremony Cap had begun.

It was a lonely life for a fellow who had been a happy family man. Except for Odessa Philmore, a friend and housekeeper, who had been sent to them by their friends the Gardeners when Bena came home with a diagnosis of cancer, Vernon was alone in the house. His married women friends, as married women are wont to do, tried their hands at matchmaking from time to time. Nothing took.

Most of them knew that he had an ill-starred friendship, mellowing into courtship and approaching marriage with an attractive Atlanta woman, widow of his friend and fellow trustee at Westminster, Malon Courts. Mr. Courts died while playing tennis at the Piedmont Driving Club in June 1957. Vernon called on his wife, Vaughn, at the time, and a couple of years after Malon's death friends began to invite them everywhere together.

It was a happy association for both of them with evenings at the opera and jolly excursions to the homes of friends in the mountains, and they soon planned to get married. Church friends who knew both of them were pleased and decided on a little announcement party to apprise the elders of the happy event.

Vaughn had been having misgivings, questioning her ability to be a minister's wife, wondering if she could possibly succeed the pretty and vivacious first wife, Bena. Vernon sensed her uncertainty, and on the eve of the engagement party he said, "You are not completely happy about this. You're free. We'll see what happens."

He went to the party. Vaughn tactfully stayed away. He went on a European trip they had planned to take together with his uncle Newell Ellison and Newell's daughter Jonnie. Later he was to tell his disappointed daughters, who admired the lovely Vaughn, that he had "let her off the hook."

They remained friends and maintained a warm and happy relationship for about a year before Vaughn was married to a charming Atlanta businessman, Frank Player.

In 1966 another attractive widow, Eloise Foster Darby, was collecting and pasting in a scrapbook Vernon's newspaper columns. She did not know him personally, although she worked in the office of his friend, President Wallace Alston, at Agnes Scott. But she had heard him speak at a meeting on the campus and admired him from afar.

A small slender woman with a flair for understated elegance in her clothes and a talent for playing the piano, Eloise had grown up in Shreveport, Louisiana, the youngest of a lawyer's five children. One of her sisters was living in Mexico City and attending the American University there. Eloise, a music major at a Louisiana Normal school, had transferred to Louisiana State University, but she decided to visit her sister and investigate the American University's music school. While she was there she met Marion Darby, an executive with the Carrier Airconditioning Corporation.

"I wasn't flying blind," she now jokes. "He had to make a trip to Rio de Janeiro and he wanted me to go with him. I wanted to go — so we were married. It was 1936 — and my first time on a plane or a ship."

When they returned Mr. Darby was offered a position with the company in Atlanta, and they moved to Decatur, where their only son, Robert Marion, was born a year later. Robert, now grown and a graduate of the United States Naval Academy at Annapolis, where he was chosen June Week Commander for his graduation week in 1959, was in the navy. Eloise had been a widow for five years when she met Vernon Broyles.

She had a niece who was a student at Westminister, and she went to hear her sing in a school program at Trinity Presbyterian Church. There was a vacant seat on the aisle, and Eloise asked the man next to it if he was saving it for somebody. He was not and she sat down.

"We shared a hymn book and I couldn't help noticing that he knew all the words without looking," she said. Later she saw Vernon's picture in the paper, and her niece confirmed that the man who knew the hymns was the chairman of her school's board of trustees.

167

Not long after that a friend wanted her to ride to the airport with her to meet someone she felt Eloise would like to know. "We were passing North Avenue church and I said lightly, 'The man I want to meet is right over there in that church!' "

Word got around. Eloise's friend mentioned it at her book club, and another member who happened to be related to Jimmie Smyth mentioned it to him at the grocery store. He told Virginia and she promptly invited them to dinner together.

Within three months Vernon was pressing for marriage. "I couldn't do it that fast. My son was in a nuclear submarine and I wanted to tell him first," Eloise said.

They were married in the chapel of Decatur Presbyterian Church with the Smyths and the children of both present. The pastor of the church, the Reverend Davidson Phillips, and Dr. Broyles's son Cap, then pastor of the Dothan, Alabama, Presbyterian church, performed the ceremony.

Vernon sold the house on The Prado where he had lived for more than twenty years. His friend, Tom Cousins, consulted as his personal expert on real estate, was amazed when Vernon got twenty-one thousand dollars for it. "He didn't think it was worth the $7,200 I paid for it in the first place," Vernon chortled.

Vernon and Eloise moved into a pretty house they rented a few blocks away on Peachtree Circle. Eloise enjoyed buying new furniture, curtains, and rugs to decorate it and had a pleasant time planning parties to reciprocate those that couples in the church were giving to celebrate their marriage. She joined in church projects, played the piano at Sunday school, and sang in the church choir.

Most of the Virden antiques that had belonged to Bena went to the children. Before his marriage and the sale of the house, Vernon had asked the three of them to make a list of the furniture they wanted, and, if they didn't get it or couldn't use it immediately, he would earmark it for them and they could claim it later. "And if there is any arguing," Betsy quoted her father as saying, "I'm calling the Salvation Army."

So far as she knew, Betsy added with a laugh, there was no arguing, and she and her second husband, Calvin Moore, continue to sleep in the heavy four-poster bed that cost the church so much to move from Mississippi.

"But without the tester," Betsy said. "My ceilings are not that high."

Remembering the portrait of her mother in her wedding gown and feeling certain her father was no longer going to keep it on his desk with a new wife around, Betsy asked for that. "I'm not ready to give that up yet," Vernon said.

Although the three young Broyleses scattered to Florida, Tennessee, and Alabama, Vernon remained close to them. He delighted in the births of grandchildren and usually made it to the hospital to greet every newborn. Aware that girls with mothers had a loving standby to see them through their first week at home with a new baby, he said apologetically, "I'm not going to do that but I want you to have somebody. Hire somebody for a week and I'll pay. But" — a last laughing warning — "it's not going to be me!"

Between them his children gave him seven grandchildren — all boys and all grown up now. One of them, Bebe's son, and his wife produced Vernon's only great-grandchild, a little boy named Edward, whom he did not live to see. Eloise's son, Robert, who retired from the navy and entered business, is counted a member of the Broyles family. He has four children.

Cap, now more generally known as the Reverend Vernon S. Broyles III, served as the pastor of Presbyterian churches in Wagram, North Carolina; Dothan, Alabama; and Montgomery, Alabama, for a number of years before he moved to Atlanta to become Director of Corporate Witness in Public Affairs for the General Assembly Mission Board. He has since moved to Louisville, where the Presbyterian General Assembly is now located. He writes a monthly column for the *Presbyterian Survey*, the denomination's magazine. Bebe, until September 1992, was assistant to the publisher of the *Memphis Business Journal*, and Betsy is a manager in a Pensacola, Florida, firm of certified public accountants.

When his daughters and son moved to a new town or a different house, Vernon made quick visits because, as he told them, "I have to visualize you where you are."

He baptized their babies, and when the families became so numerous they overflowed his and Eloise's house, he rented nearby houses or apartments to accommodate them during the frequent summertime reunions in the mountains.

Vernon felt himself to be particularly blessed in the people his children married and in their offspring. George Cates, to whom Bebe was married shortly after her graduation from Emory University, was particularly close and dear to his heart. George became enmeshed in the family the summer of Bena's final illness. Bebe, his betrothed, was on a trip to Europe, and young Cates assigned himself the role of visiting her mother every day and standing by when Vernon might need him. A highly successful Memphis businessman, he was later to supply his father-in-law with cars from time to time.

The summer before his death Vernon was driving a BMW. "Every country preacher needs a car like this," he joked. "But you have to have a son-in-law like mine."

Betsy's first marriage ended in divorce — a matter of distress to her father. "There was nothing judgmental in that," his younger daughter recalled. "I think it was just concern for my happiness and security. He was pleased when I was dating Cal (Calvin Moore), but I think he was quite concerned when I married him because he knew him so little and therefore had no basis for knowing it was a good thing."

Betsy and Cal were married two years before Vernon's death, time for the minister and his son-in-law to establish a close and satisfying friendship.

Several months before his death Vernon spent Thanksgiving with Cal's family on a farm they own in Alabama. He wrote Bebe afterwards that the Moores "could not have been more gracious in their hospitality" and he was pleased that they had included Cap with Betsy and Cal. "I continued to be amazed at Cal and his reception of our family. He and Betsy appear to bring to one another real fulfillment."

Vernon was pleased at Cal's feeling for Betsy's sons by her first marriage, and another evidence of "God's providence" in his affairs came triumphantly to mind following Tom's graduation from Emory that December.

"He was 23," Betsy said of her son, "and he had no idea what he was going to do when he graduated. He was looking for direction and went up one Saturday in the fall to have lunch with Daddy and just talk about it. The director of sales there was John Thomas. He and Daddy had planned to have lunch that day, so Daddy just included Tom. It was totally unplanned but went well. Several weeks later John called Daddy and asked what Tom's plans were. Daddy told him that Tom was looking for a job, and John asked that Tom come to see him."

The upshot was that the Big Canoe developer had a post for Tom, and best of all, to Betsy and to Vernon himself, was that Tom moved in with him and Eloise — in much the same way that he had found a home with his father and stepmother, Martha, during the uncertain days following his own graduation from college.

"There developed between Tom and Eloise a special affection," Betsy said. "She was wonderful to him and I hope enjoyed him as much as he enjoyed her. Daddy was particularly grateful for this. Tom visited Daddy at the start of each day and at its end. He listened to their scripture, devotionals, and prayers after breakfast. Daddy declared him a 'splendid' young man and an unexpectedly wonderful addition. I believe his life will be forever different for the short time he spent there."

After his grandfather died, Tom stayed on to keep Eloise company and help her through the inevitable agony of loneliness and adjustment. Later the family was to remember that

Dr. Broyles "felt that in a very real way he was repaying a debt he owed to Martha" in his and Eloise's welcoming Tom.

10

Death is a basic fact of our experience and at the same time life's greatest mystery. We are not free to live until we have to some extent freed ourselves of the fear of death.

VSB letter to E.P.

Death might have been considered Vernon's constant and unrelenting adversary. He faced it himself in Bena's death and he faced it almost daily with some member of his congregation. He sat at the bedside of the dying. He walked the halls with the bereaved. Hardly a month went by but that he was called upon to officiate at the funeral and stand at the graveside of somebody he cared about.

Far from facing it with sad resignation, he plumbed the depths of the mystery and came to believe that it was a positive thing, useful and natural if inevitable.

"I have found," he wrote a young woman

who asked, "loss of that which is most dear to you and moving forward with the sheer courage of daring to believe will make one a more useful person in the relationships of his or her life. I became a far more useful pastor after I had gone through deep waters and appeared—outwardly at least—to be able to swim."

Those closest to him had no doubt that Vernon was "able to swim." Even as he approached his nineties he was deeply involved in the lives of many, many people. Eloise was often ill, and he took on little household chores from time to time, taking pleasure in preparing their meals and even making jelly when fruit ripened in the mountains in the late summer.

He followed the habit of a lifetime by beginning every day with Bible reading and prayer, reading a Spanish Bible to strengthen his knowledge of the language. His study on the ground floor of the mountain house was a light-filled room with a constantly changing panoramic view of the hill country. Around him were the books and family mementoes he loved—his mother's scrapbook, the battered little Teddy bear that he had cherished since childhood, keeping it on a shelf in his study when he was at home, tucking it in his suitcase when he traveled, and the pictures of children and grandchildren. Here he sat and silently prayed for an amazing list of people, recent acquaintances and old friends he hadn't seen in years, troubled ones and young ones embarking on new adventures. He never forgot because he kept a "prayer list" of more than a hundred names.

He had a typewriter and he maintained the skill of his college days by answering personally a great many letters. Some of these concerned faith. Many concerned death.

To a young woman who asked for "coping advice" when she should lose her mother and even him, her friend and counsellor, he cited Heb. 2:15, which speaks of them who fear death as being "all their lifetime subject to bondage." "Facing it as a fact of life," he wrote, "is comparable to facing the dark, which can do much to remove the fear of the dark."

And then: "The Christian faith presents death as an event in God's continuing plan and providence. It is not the end but a new beginning to which we commit our loved ones. All peoples in all periods of history have intuitively believed this and the Christian faith meets this intuition with the resurrection of ONE PERSON who said that because He lives we shall live also."

A sense of loss and grief, he continued, should not be evaded or hidden because, "being natural, they are a healing experience." Going ahead with your life and "daring to believe that God is in control" is not always easy, he admitted, "but it is possible and the best that I know."

The activities around the Big Canoe Chapel were endlessly engrossing to him. As the beautiful little "church in the wildwood" (it adopted an old hymn by that name as its theme song) grew, a fellowship hall seemed to be needed for meetings, dinners, and even exercise classes. The hall was built and dedicated as the Broyles Community Center. As usual, Vernon was given credit by the workers for seeing it through, although, unlike former President Jimmy Carter, he did not pick up a hammer.

"I thought being retired meant playing golf, relaxing, sitting around and rocking on the porch," said Beverly White, activities director at Big Canoe. "This man was working so hard. He has tackled problems that no one else would have touched, some involved employees' problems. If he felt he needed to talk to the management of Big Canoe he would do that also, always making a difference."

Mrs. White said she had never seen Dr. Broyles without a smile on his face. When she mentioned that, Vernon laughed and told her the story of the little girl who asked her mother if she was happy. "Yes!" snapped the mother, and the child replied, "Well, you should tell your face."

It was a favorite little sermonette for a man who seldom told jokes, and never from the pulpit. He did smile a lot and his explosive laughter came often and easily, but he was not a humorous preacher who laced his sermons with funny stories. When he entered the pulpit he was grave and dignified, clearly feeling the sanctity of the time and place and caught up in the vital message he hoped to bring.

Many of Vernon's sermons never reached the pulpit. For the elderly and infirm and people who simply wanted them to read and reread, the church printed on the front page of its weekly bulletin mini-sermons of four or five hundred words. They went into the homes of most of the members and were often asked for by non-members.

For young people he gave four special

sermons intended to instruct and enlighten those who contemplated marriage. The church brought out the four in a booklet called "Looking Toward Marriage," and it was widely distributed to couples who sought counselling, even by other ministers in other denominations. The first sermon spoke of marriage as "a miracle of God, not a human contract" easily dissolved.

"The Church has always resisted divorce," he said, "because you cannot separate two people who once have been married." There are exceptions in Scripture when divorce is acceptable, he continued, "but there are very few of them. If men and women who marry recognized this fact of a binding together in this indissoluble unity of two lives and if it were not possible to get divorces, most people who now get divorces would continue to live together fairly happily."

"I am thoroughly romantic about this thing called marriage," he said. "I know there is nothing on earth like the joy of being happily married, watching it grow, enjoying its growth through the years. I covet it for every person but I know that unless people of like faith are yoked together it cannot work." He cited statistics showing that people who profess no faith have the highest rate of divorce, and where there is a religiously mixed marriage the ratio of divorce is almost equally high. When couples of the same faith — either Catholic or Protestant — marry, the divorce rate is far lower, slightly above six percent for both denominations, as compared to fifteen and sixteen percent for non-believers and mixed faiths.

He ended that sermon with the assurance that people entering marriage as a Christian commitment could handle the problems that would inevitably arise. "As you look toward marriage," he told the young people, "I commend you to Christ."

Later when two of his children, Betsy and Cap, were divorced, he was saddened by it, but he said little. "There were a lot of things he opposed in principle," said Cap, "but he never lost sight of the people involved, and he rarely came down on them in a judgmental way."

11

> *Without murmuring, in His
> hand leave whatever things thou canst not
> understand.*
>
> **VSB scrapbook**

If he thought about it at all, Vernon
Broyles did not consider himself a pioneer
type. He enjoyed the out-of-doors, but a well-
groomed golf course and an occasional picnic struck him as sufficient. He was not a
hewer of wood or a toter of water, despite his
country beginnings.

But there are people who will say that with
his adventurous spirit, his indestructible op-
timism, his cheerful energy, and his infec-
tious faith, the great west would have been
won in half the time. An amazing North Georgia wild mountain mecca that is now home to
six hundred human households and un-
counted bear and deer is the proof.

One day in 1974, Vernon and Eloise took
a picnic lunch and fared forth to the North

Georgia mountains to look for a spot to build a retirement home when he should bow out of North Avenue church in a couple of years. They went to a development called Bent Tree, which was just getting underway, and rode around looking at the building sites that were offered for sale. They found trees and a view they liked very much, and they spread their lunch and rested and dreamed a bit before they made up their minds. Before they got back to Atlanta, Vernon had written a check as down payment and mailed it.

The next day he decided to check his rash impulse for practicality with his developer friend Tom Cousins. "What did you do that for?" Tom demanded. "I've got seven thousand acres next door to Bent Tree and I'll GIVE you a lot!"

Chastened, Vernon got his earnest money back, and he and Eloise went back to the mountains, this time to the virtually impenetrable wilderness an advertising agency with a flair for Indian names had christened Big Canoe. There were some lakes, an attractive golf course under construction, a pair of lonesome rock chimneys, and a barnlike structure that had been converted into a habitation.

They heard the story of how this beautiful land had once been part of the vast acreage owned by the Tate family, founders of Georgia Marble Company. The chimneys were lone reminders of the handsome Tate home that had stood there. Hunters and hikers occasionally ran up on the rusting remains of abandoned moonshine whiskey stills. Deaths in the family and heavy taxes had caused a surviving widow to offer the wilderness to Tom Cousins.

Tom was busy with other enterprises and wasn't particularly interested, but he went to look at the land. Before he had time to shore up his resistance he had lost his heart to it.

"Tom had a dream," said John Thomas, who worked with the developer. "Vernon came to share it. And the rest of us....Well, we could see impossible obstacles but we became infected too."

Tom's dream was to make it a refuge for city people who wanted to get away from the city—either as a retirement home or as a serene woodland enclave from which commuting to Atlanta would be an easy hour's drive. He foresaw rugged earth-colored houses of wood and stone blending into the woods so artfully that hardly a stone or a leaf was disturbed. Access would be by inconspicuous country roads dipping into the valleys and riding the ridges and hill tops, curving leafy lanes that would submerge travelers in beauty. He would preserve four hundred acres for what he called "Nature Valley," a refuge for wildlife where rhododendron and mountain laurel grew and little creeks rushed over rocky passes and fell in shining waterfalls. He would build around the old Tate homesite a restaurant that would feature the old stone fireplaces and would be called The Chimneys.

And if Vernon Broyles moved there, Tom wanted a chapel, maybe gracing the highest hill. Vernon did take Tom's offer of a lot—four acres with a view of the tallest mountain in the area and a shining little lake. But he didn't agree to Tom's notion of a chapel on a distant hill. It should be in the heart of the little village that was growing to include a post office, a country store, and a meeting place.

"He was right," said Tom. "I wanted the chapel because of him. I knew when he retired and moved to the country he would die without work he loved and believed in. Putting it in the center of the community was exactly right."

Members of North Avenue church built the Broyleses' house as a gift to their retiring pastor. The Big Canoe Corporation gave the land for the chapel and would have financed the building, but Vernon had a better idea. "Raising the money won't be hard to do," he said. "And if the Big Canoe people give the money it will be THEIR chapel."

Vernon retired from North Avenue Presbyterian Church in 1976, but he had already signed on as chaplain-adviser for the building of the Big Canoe Chapel. When he and Eloise moved to the house on Petit Ridge, two young workers on the Big Canoe project had already laid the groundwork for a place for regular worship. Sam Rothermel and Floyd Blackwell had started holding Bible reading and prayer services, as John Robert Smith wrote in *Church in the Wildwood*, "on mountain tops and in valleys, at lakesides and by flowing streams, under trees and under sky." Sometimes as few as five people would be present, sometimes a goodly crowd.

The deed to the Big Canoe Chapel site was given to the Big Canoe property owners, and during the ground-breaking ceremony for the new chapel, Vernon Broyles manned the shovel. "We are involved here," he was quoted by Dr. John Robert Smith as saying, "in the most important building at Big Canoe since its beginning."

There were times, John Thomas said, when funds ran low and builders grew discouraged, but Vernon kept everybody's spirits up with his insistence that the chapel would be finished and Big Canoe itself would go on to be the "paradise" that had been envisioned for commuters and vacationers from all over the South.

"Vernon was a realist," said John Thomas, "but he always talked about how things could be made better—good, in fact. He kept everybody going because he believed in the Big Canoe dream and he made us believe in it. Turned out he was right."

John, himself, went on to other land development, but when he was ready to get married he insisted that his bride and her parents and their friends come down from North Carolina for Vernon to perform the ceremony in the Big Canoe Chapel. "There's just one man in one place I want to marry me," he said, and his bride graciously assented.

The chapel itself is, as Vernon had hoped, in the heart of the settlement in a valley, but set on a ridge with a view through its tall, clear glass windows of an even deeper valley, and beyond that Sanderlin mountain, the most southern peak in the Appalachian range. To match its "church in the wildwood" style the accouterments of the chapel have been designed by local artists and produced by local artisans.

Deanie and Bob Platt were responsible for having the offering plates hand turned by Ed Moulthrop out of native tulipwood. The communion service was wrought from Georgia clay. The baptismal font is a hand-thrown pottery bowl resting on a walnut stand. A tapestry wall hanging, given by Vernon's daughters in his honor, was handwoven by Margaret Mott, an artist who spent three days at Big Canoe deciding on her palette by collecting sample colors from the surrounding woods and hills.

The first service in the chapel was slated for Christmas Eve, 1977, and took place after a dizzying week of delays in which everybody but Vernon despaired of making the deadline. A bell, wrought by the same VanBergen family who cast the North Avenue bell, seemed destined to remain on the ground while workmen struggled to get the belfry in position. But it was in place and ready to ring out Christmas tidings that night, and has rung since then on Sunday mornings and at vesper time.

Vernon had been conducting services at several makeshift sites, but that night with candlelight glowing against the stone walls, he recited the Christmas story in a real and very beautiful church.

He was to continue as chaplain, alternating with other ministers for Sunday services until February 1992, when he preached his last sermon. He was very proud of an interdenominational congregation which, he bragged, "includes a Roman Catholic, a Jew, some Southern Baptists, and, of course, Presbyterians, Episcopalians, and Methodists."

The range of faiths represented was to grow when the Reverend Wayne Smith of the Friendship Force started bringing in people from other lands, including Soviet dignitaries, who were accompanied by then President Jimmy and Mrs. Carter.

From time to time Vernon had received a merry, convivial measure of his congregation's affection for him. In 1957 the people of North Avenue had staged a gala "This Your Life" performance, secretly bringing in friends and relatives from the past, including his sister Elizabeth Hargen of Monroe, Louisiana, and his uncle Newell Ellison of Washington, to tell amusing and outrageous stories about him and to give him a new automobile. He kept a massive scrapbook of the letters and cards he received and the photographs taken at the party.

Later Big Canoe friends "roasted" him with a gala mountain birthday party at which there was picking and singing and clog dancers and acres of home-cooked food.   There were a lot of gags and jokes at his expense, but Ann Cousins created one that had a fine shock value and a lot of hilarity accompanying it. To rival Bert Reynolds, who a few months before had appeared as a centerfold of *Cosmopolitan Magazine*, she made her minister the nude centerfold of *Cosmopolitan* with a double-page photograph of him naked—at age three months.

Vernon's eightieth birthday in 1984 was a real occasion for his friends to express themselves tearfully, humorously, with unabashed sentimentality. Naturally glad that he had lived so long, they let themselves go by writing him love letters. He saved them all in fat leather binders.

President Reagan, former President Carter, and then Georgia Governor Joe Frank Harris were more formal in their words of appreciation for his life of service. Jimmie

Smyth, his old friend from Canton, was exuberant. He cited the four decades they had been friends with exclamation marks and said, "You are the Best man I have ever known, the Best preacher I have ever heard and the Best friend I have ever had."

Bill Flinn, the son of Dr. Flinn, and his wife Elizabeth, author of the North Avenue history, *With Feet of Clay*, wrote a five stanza poem, ending,

> Well will we remember each private
>   little thing
> Which friend to friend relationships can
>   almost always bring;
> You welcomed all our newborn
>   babes and prayed when we were ill.
> You charmed our aging parents and
>   they loved you with good will;
> You comforted our sorrow and you
>   laughed with us in joy.
> We cherish you this special day, dear
>   friend and birthday boy.

Attorney Franklin Bloodworth was reared in North Avenue church, and he was a little boy of five or six when Vernon arrived. He recounted that his family made him go to church, and when Dr. Broyles began his sermon the little boy took it as the signal to get a piece of paper out of the pew rack and start drawing pictures. When he got to be eight years old, his father leaned over and whispered, "You are old enough now to pay attention. Put up your pencil and start listening."

"And I have been listening ever since!" the lawyer exclaimed.

Martine Joyner, member of a founding North Avenue family, and an artist, resorted to free verse, beginning "Dear Long Time Friend, What new wish can be given for your birthday? Well, you have never been 80 before so I'll try."

May your life be as long as your
     patience
with the hundreds of sheep you
     shepherd.
May your health be as good as that of
     the young man
who came to North Avenue as Pastor
     when I was also young.
May your peace be as deep as the love
     your many friends feel for you.
May your joy be as high as the
     mountains which surround you.
May God's hand uphold you as you
     have upheld others.
May your blessings be more than
     80-fold.

Wilhelmina and Campbell McKay, stalwart members of his pastorate at North Avenue from the beginning, quoted Psalms: "Thy youth is renewed like the eagle's on high by the Lord of the heavens, the earth and the sky."

Harllee Branch, Jr., Atlanta businessman and a fellow student at Davidson College, recalled that Vernon displayed "outstanding scholarship and a truly unique ability to get things done" even then. He spoke of their work together on the college paper, when he had decided that Vernon would be one of the nation's leading businessmen "but rejoiced, as did many others, when you decided to devote your life to the ministry."

Paul Duke, a real estate developer and elder in the church, wrote, "You occupy a special place in my heart because you are the only person in this world, outside of my wife, who has accepted me 'for better or for worse.' I feel that you are blessed with a true touch of greatness enjoyed by few."

A ninety-year-old woman remembered the sound of his joyful laughter. She recited the names of four generations of her family who were members of his church. A secretary remembered that he whistled in the hall.

"In our times of trouble, heartache or sadness you have provided counsel and love...and given us courage," wrote one couple. "Your faith and Biblical teaching have brought us through."

Vernon loved the day, the feast under the tent enfolded in November's blaze of color, and he loved evidences of friendship. Hundreds of letters and cards came to him, and he kept them on a shelf in the comfortable study with its windows looking out on the valley and its little deck where he liked to sit and read on good days.

He may have read and reread all of those messages of love, but there was one in the front of the looseleaf folder that must have especially pleased him when his eyes took it in.

It began, "Dear Daddy" and it was from his younger daughter Betsy. "As a child I assumed that everyone had a father like you. It wasn't until I went off to college that I began to appreciate your uniqueness. As I have grown older that realization has grown.

"You've given us unstintingly of your time, love and support. You've given advice only when we've asked for it, and never, ever any criticism. As a parent myself I think that may be the hardest part.

"The love is everything. I love you more than you'll ever know."

A letter from Betsy's first husband, Tommy Grimes, invariably brought a grin to Vernon's face because he had quoted Vernon's own recipe for longevity, which he had given his grandsons: "Don't die."

The Canton Presbyterian Church celebrated its 150th anniversary in 1987, and Vernon went back to make what he called "a satisfying walk down memory lane." Bebe and her family met him there, taking two cars and persuading him to drive back to Memphis in one of them with her sons, whose company he valued.

"It meant a great deal that the Cateses were there," he later wrote Betsy, "It gave their boys a glimpse of their roots."

For himself an hour's walk about the little town was sad. He missed the bustle that he had known around the square. (Mosby's Drug store was the only store he remembered that was still open for business.) But he enjoyed getting reacquainted with the sons and daughters of old friends —"men and women forty-five to fifty years old — who were children and young people when last I saw them, and their long-gone families came to life."

"I felt at home in the pulpit there, and it was a good service," he wrote. "The church is alive and doing well. It has a good many young couples providing leadership."

Elise Priestly Hinton, Bena's first cousin, and her husband, had the family to lunch in the old white-columned house on Fulton Street, where he had lived as a bachelor and courted the Virden girl in the house beyond the back garden.

He might have remembered that just as his children worried about a swarm of bees that inhabited one of the white columns across the front when they visited the house, Bena, in her girlhood, had mused about the ghosts that dwelled in that house and in the house belonging to her parents beyond the garden. In her diary she had written poetically of hearing her little brother, Percy, who was five when he died, asking for a teacake, of her father sitting in his old rocker reading western stories, and of a dashing Confederate ancestor in a plumed hat, probably the one whose painted eyes in an oil portrait in the parlor followed little children when they moved through the house.

They weren't his ghosts. But he must have had others more poignant. "It was an emotional, stirring experience," he wrote. "Every corner of the house brought back memories."

A stopover in Memphis on the way home cheered and refreshed him. He spent several days in Memphis with Bebe and her family, and Vernon particularly enjoyed getting acquainted with his grandsons and visiting them at their homes and offices. They even took time to revisit the newly restored Peabody Hotel and watch the famous ducks make their trek across the lobby to the pool where they disported in the daytime.

Back at Big Canoe, Vernon returned to the duties that normally engrossed him— preaching twice a month and attending meetings in the Broyles Community Center. He always had funerals and weddings on his agenda, and he performed these services willingly, with the exception of one.

A young couple called to ask him to marry them in the beautiful Big Canoe Chapel, and he would be glad to do it, after the requisite counselling session. But when they showed up with a trick dog they had trained to serve as ring bearer he balked. He liked dogs very much, and he always stopped to speak to them in the road, but a performing dog had no place in what he considered a very sacred ceremony. The young couple took their trick dog and went elsewhere.

Friends and family who had regarded Vernon as indestructible, couldn't help but notice that he was tiring. His smooth dark hair had long since turned white. His handsome face was furrowed. He gave up golf, which had kept him out-of-doors for many enjoyable hours. His clubs stood in a corner in the front hall of his house, and when he passed them he would lay a finger on the slender shaft of a driver and say whimsically, "No more."

In February of 1992, he told the board of trustees, the ruling body of the Big Canoe Chapel, that he wanted to retire. But Franklin Bloodworth, whom he had asked the previous fall to chair the 1992 Big Canoe World Missions Conference, persuaded him to wait until after the conference, which was set for the last weekend in March, to retire. One of Vernon's dreams was to start such a conference at Big Canoe. More than thirty years earlier, Vernon had persuaded North Avenue Presbyterian Church to start a mission conference, and over the years, the conference had grown to be one of the most important parts of the Atlanta church's ministry. In fact, Vernon had told Franklin, "If I can help establish such a conference at Big Canoe, that will be my most important contribution to the Chapel." Vernon agreed to continue and to retire on April 1, after the World Mission Conference had concluded.

Franklin elicited another promise from him. He wanted once more to hear Vernon preach what the Bloodworths called his "keep on keeping on" sermon. They had illness in the family and anxious times, and they drew strength and courage from his assurances that there is hope, and even a certain glory in the dogged business of "putting one foot ahead of the other."

On Sunday, February 9, Vernon preached his last sermon. It was on "keep on keeping on" and the thing that makes it possible—hope.

He spoke of the natural phenomena over which man has no control, the rising and setting of the sun, the miracle of life in a seed, the mysteries of the human body, which medicine can tinker with but cannot create.

"Nobody on earth knows why the heart keeps beating," he said. "It just keeps on keeping on. And there's the eye. An eye surgeon told me that if anybody could study the structure of the human eye and not believe in a creator, it was beyond his understanding. He went on to the topic of healing and said that doctors can "remove the obstacles," but that "no doctor, no physician ever healed anybody."

An even more miraculous phenomenon, he said, is hope. "One of the strangest things in the human heart is hope" he said, citing refugees who trudge along with their possessions in little packs on their backs, propelled by hope of a better place, a better life.

Without hope he said, they "would sit down and claw the ground in despair," but with hope "they just keep on putting one foot ahead of the other."

To the poet Emily Dickinson hope was "the thing with feathers/ That perches in the soul,/ And sings the tune without the words/ And never stops at all."

The source of this singing bird to Vernon Broyles was two of his best-loved passages of scripture, which he recited to people he loved for the last time:

From Corinthians: "And he said unto me, My grace is sufficient unto thee; for my strength is made perfect in weakness."

From Romans: "For I am persuaded that neither death, nor life, nor angels nor principalities, nor powers, nor things present, nor things to come, nor height, nor depth, nor any other creature, shall be able to separate us from the love of God, which is in Christ Jesus our Lord."

Three days after preaching this sermon, Vernon lay near death in Atlanta's Crawford Long Hospital. Two of the city's finest heart surgeons told him his eighty-seven-year-old heart was simply worn out and probably could not be repaired, but if he so desired, they were willing to try. Always with hope, Vernon replied, "Let's try! This will be another great adventure for me."

On February 13, 1992, Vernon Seba Broyles, Jr., began his last and greatest adventure.

AFTERWORD

In October 1960 the *Atlanta Constitution* announced in a quarter-page house ad the start of three inspirational columns. They were to be written by Dr. Robert V. Ozmont, pastor of the First Methodist Church; Dr. Roy O. McClain, pastor of the First Baptist Church; and Dr. Broyles.

In an effort to bring readers "the finest inspirational writing and to offer a broader perspective," said the ad, "the *Constitution* is justifiably proud of the addition of these three ministers to its columns."

For four years Dr. Broyles wrote two opposite editorial-page columns twice a week addressing deepest human spiritual needs and aspirations.

He began with the topic of insecurity, the effort of mankind to find "a firm footing in life." He passed over money, health, and family relationships as deeply coveted but not dependable things. Instead he listed for his readers "the firm supports" available to them:

obedience to conscience, kindness, church worship, and faithfulness to God.

The following paragraphs amount to arbitrary condensations from many columns.

CONSCIENCE

Conscience says to each of us, "I ought-or ought not." It pronounces you guilty when you disobey it and you get a glimpse of true goodness when you obey. Conscience speaks with authority because it is the authority of God.

PEACE IN HARDSHIP

God promises no man an easy life. In Christ he invites you to take up your cross and obey Him. He promises that His strength shall be sufficient. God never offers us freedom from storm but guarantees for us a stout ship, a good compass and a harbor at last. Peace in a storm, a song at midnight, a cry of victory in the face of death—these are the marks of faith.

BELIEF

If you believe that God rules this world you will be able to live in it without fear. It makes a difference if you believe in God to whom you are personally morally responsible. It makes a difference if you know God loves you in spite of your sin. It is easy to become discouraged and even cynical but it makes a difference in our fight to really believe that the victory of God over evil is already assured.

SIN

We are all sinners. No day passes but that we sin in some way. Now the heart of the gospel is that Christ came to save sinners. To the dismay of the "important" people of His day he spent the greater part of his ministry with those of ill repute.

WEARINESS

It was man's first sin in Eden that he decided to go it alone. We still sin Adam's sin and we still suffer Adam's penalty—weariness and disaster. We are not made to go it alone. It is not easy to believe God nor is it easy to trust Him. But it is the only way to escape that day when you will say with my friend, "I am the tiredest man you ever saw."

MARRIAGE

If you have happiness, treasure it. If it has slipped away seek it with all your heart.

RELIGION

A man's religion makes him what he is. Faithfulness, honesty, patience, consideration, loyalty, courage, wisdom do not just happen. They are the fruits of character. Character is the result of man's religion. It determines how he pays his bills, how faithful he is to his marriage vows. It sets the whole moral tone of his life. Religion matters so much that all efforts to reform men or society will fail unless they begin with each man's personal relation to God, which is his religion.

CHURCH BUILDING

The church building is a silent sentinel keeping guard over the best that is within us. By its very presence it reminds us that to do right is better than to do wrong, to act kindly is finer than to hurt another, to live purely is better than to soil our lives. When you see a church building take heart. As long as men build churches faith lives. As long as faith lives evil that seems so strong will be defeated.

KEEPING THE SABBATH

How to keep the day? First, it is the Lord's day, the day on which he was raised from the dead. It is a weekly reminder that someone died for us. Second, it is a day simply of rest. Third, it is a day for the home, a day when in which through some joint activity the family may be found together. Fourth, it is a day of worship when believers worshipping together experience the power of God. Fifth, it is a day for doing good, a day in which, within the circle of your life, a kind word or deed by you makes the difference in the entire outlook of somebody else. In keeping the Lord's day we find stability for the other six days and it is through the loyalty of the people who keep it that God will save our day and give us a better tomorrow.

SELF DESTRUCTION

There is a peculiar twist in human nature that makes us go on destroying ourselves. We want to be happy and we do things to make it impossible. We want to be useful and helpful and persist in being self-centered. We are sharp with our loved ones when we mean to be gentle. We nag when we know we should encourage. We win love by thoughtfulness and kindness and lose it by selfishness and harshness. We act cold and distant when our hearts cry out for warmth and affection. In many a heart there is the cry of the apostle Paul, "Who shall deliver me from the body of this death?" There is only one answer: "I thank God through Jesus Christ our Lord."

FAITH AND CHANGE

There are personal problems, political problems, problems in the church—and there are enough Christians in Atlanta alone to revolutionize the whole world. Yet we are not changing life around us. Read the New Testament. Peter had sickness in the family. Paul was physically handicapped. They spent a good bit of time in jail. They saw members of their family killed because they were Christians. They had slavery. They had poverty. They had immorality. Their land was occupied by foreigners. Yet one finds no discussion of these problems running through the New Testament. It was the simple story of people on the march—out to do something. They started out to change the world with no resources as we count such things. They had only an absolute personal conviction that Jesus was the Son of God...and that there was no answer unless Christ was in the center. Don't dismiss them as flighty idealists. Everything that is dear in our civilization stems from these foolish men and women who went forth—starting with 120—witnessing to this conviction.

LENT

The Lenten season has a strange place in our modern world. Lent speaks of suffering and death. We seek to escape suffering and ignore death as best we can. Lent tells of earthly failure as the door to heavenly treasure while we strive only for earthly success. Lent speaks of saving yourself by losing yourself and we have no intention of getting lost in the shuffle if we can help it. Lent speaks of living and growing in the world of the spirit while we think of growth in terms of statistics. Lent speaks of the eternal value of the least persons while we think of prestige and position. Lent speaks of how God sent His Son to redeem and save us and we think we can do it ourselves. We do well in this season quietly to ponder the message of Lent.

KNOWING WHY

If these words can encourage a few of us to face squarely the question of why we are doing whatever we are doing and to follow where it leads they will not be in vain. The degree of business and social success has little to do with whether a person feels useful or useless. Money is a poor cover for an empty heart. People of the empty heart are usually busy people. They are often kind people.

There is nothing wrong with them as neighbors and citizens except that they have no answer to the question, "Why?" The truth is such people have never really had the courage to face God honestly. Each human being is made so that he doesn't function properly unless his first interest is to glorify God and to enjoy Him now and forever. Devoting himself and his talents to the glory of God, he that has received much will give much and in his giving find the answer to the question, "Why am I doing what I am doing?"

COOL, CALM, COLLECTED

The question of how to stay cool, calm, and collected was asked by some philosophers and psychologists. Philosophy or psychology cut loose from God is just play acting. It results in wisdom that becomes foolish. We need more than will power. The whole impact of the Christian faith is toward giving us direction, purpose, and power. By faith we are so related to God that His power comes through to us. That is why the question is ever a religious one and my answer must seek its roots in the grace of God.

PRAYER

Prayer is [an] agonizing experience. It is

dealing with the great spiritual currents of our world. Prayer is putting yourself in tune with the spiritual powers of God. It is a dangerous and thrilling thing to do. It requires commitment. We must come to prayer expecting an answer. If you really pray out of need, out of surrender, you are going to get an answer. If you really seek God's will for your life and your world, you are going to get an answer. God bids us to expect an answer.

EVANGELISM

How often in the past month have you gone to anyone in trouble or in sin and told them that you have something in your faith that will answer their need? We are hesitant to go to the alcoholic or gossip or thief and offer Christ as the answer. We work up enthusiasm over our old school ties and let everyone know where we stand. How does anyone know you are a Christian?

The early Christians did not have education, they had passion. They had a story to tell that had changed their lives from hopelessness to hope, from slavery to freedom, from sin to salvation. They had found peace for the heart though their lives were marked by suffering and death. We cannot expect a lost world to take us seriously unless we give evidence of a faith that shows the passion of personal commitment.

FAITH AND COURAGE

Often our chief need is just courage and strength to go on bearing our burdens. It is remarkable how often faith in God's presence, however weak the faith may seem, becomes the means by which we receive courage to go on. For those who dare to believe and dare to go on there comes a better day. The situation does not always change. Sometimes it gets worse. But there comes strength for the day and always finally comes God's answer.

PATIENCE

Paul says that he has found certain wonderful results in the troubles in his life. By his troubles he learned patience. Patience is something we all recommend and which usually is practiced and learned under necessity. It is a golden virtue. It is enduring under strain and standing fast under testing. Only as we are tested and find ourselves standing up under it do we come to know we can take it.

BURDENS

If your burdens are too heavy, check and

see if you are living in love with God and with your friends and family and associates. If you are cut off by your neglect or by your selfishness, you will fall under your burdens. Only as God's strength can come to you as you open your heart in response to his love and to that of your fellows, can your spirit and body be constantly refreshed for the tasks of the day.

KEEPING THE SABBATH

I am writing another column on keeping holy to God one day in seven because of a deep conviction that it is necessary if we are to find strength, if we are to realize our divine potential. You must include at least four features: 1. Worship. 2. Rest. 3. Time for the family. 4. Deeds of love and mercy. A day of rest was here long before Moses. The Code of Hammurabi—six hundred years before Moses and two thousand years before Christ—has as its very heart the keeping of one day in seven holy unto their God. Voltaire, who was never a friend of Christianity, said that any man who would destroy Christianity would first have to destroy the Christian sabbath. Disraeli, a great English statesman and a Jew, said "the Christian sabbath is the cornerstone of civilization." We don't have an opinion about keeping the sabbath. It is a

217

necessity if the church is to last.

TOO BUSY

We often take for granted that if we are busy, all is well. Our most precious possessions are crowded out beyond recall before we are aware of what is happening. The only way out is to face honestly the question as to what is really important to you and then having the courage to give the important things first place in the use of your time and energy. Our two most precious possessions are God's love in Christ and human love in those who care. Put them first in your time and in the spending of your energy. You will be happier and, strangely enough, you will be more useful.

GOD'S WILL

In any serious discussion of prayer we are usually reminded that we must enclose our praying with the words, "Thy will be done." Especially is this true when we are in the midst of some emergency which is beyond our strength to handle. There are times when circumstances make our hands grow weak and our hearts become faint within us. We reach out after God with our requests for help. We are so sure we know what we need that we are confused by the petition, "thy will be done." It is not a cry of resignation nor just making the best of a situation. To say "Thy will be done" is to make the grand surrender to one who loves you and who is able and willing to help you.

GOOD AND BAD

So much emphasis is put on the bad things in our lives we tend to grow too discouraged about the good. Certain facts need to be remembered: 1. There is evil all through our world, but there is also good. We need to be reminded that the world belongs to God and to the good. 2. The good grows and multiplies. 3. Evil is always self-destructive. Leave it alone and it shows itself for what it is. 4. Life moves toward a final accounting when the victory of good will be manifest in God's last judgement. Then evil will reach its final end and be cast out forever.

FORGIVENESS

The world is being driven to bankruptcy making bombs. We are having trouble winning and keeping friends. Mental illness is a national problem. Crime is flourishing. The world is an armed camp. The majority of the peoples of the world live in police states. Most of these problems go back to people who live with unforgiving spirits. Hate and hostility poison our best efforts. You can't solve the world's problems, but you can begin their solution with yourself. God offers you forgiveness....You must forgive those who have trespassed against you.

BAD TIMES

Things can go terribly wrong. In a moment of agony it helps to admit frankly that there is no satisfying answer in the situation, that pain and sorrow happen to everyone, and to ask the question, "What would God have me do with my pain?" Surrender yourself and your pain to God, daring to believe that He will take care of you and use you and your loss for some constructive purpose. Then just ask God to show you what to do next and keep on doing what appears as the next thing to do.

LIFE'S SHAPE

Believing yourself supported by God, you can meet heavy responsibility with the assurance, "I can do all things through Christ who gives me strength." You can meet trouble with the support, "If God can be for us, who can be against us." You can meet sorrow with comfort: "My peace I give unto you." If you believe the right things about God, you will believe the right things about yourself and all you need will be added unto you.

GRADUATES

Hold on to your dreams, young graduates. Cryers of doom are on every hand. The forces of God are stronger than the forces of evil. In this confidence you can take your next step. Happiness lies in following your dreams in faith, perseverance, and integrity. There may be a painful delay. At times it will seem that surely all dreams die and evil always wins. But hold on to your dreams. The future is in God's hands and he has promised the victory to those who in faith dream great dreams.

HELP IN DESPERATION

Commit yourself to spend time each day reading the Bible a minimum of one-half hour but preferably one hour. Read it as you would any other book. Read it without any concern about what you believe or do not believe, just read it with one prayer: "God, if you are in it, and have anything to say to me, point it out to me." You will know when there is a word for you. Don't try to make anything happen. Just let it happen. Start with reading John's gospel and read it twice. Then read the Psalms. Then the prophet Isaiah. Memorize some passages where you have concerns, some of it will pop into your mind. Suggestions: Matthew 6:31-34; Psalms 23, 1, 341-10; John 14:25-27; Philippians 4:4-7.

Then go somewhere to church each Sunday—and this again with an open mind, just with the prayer that if God has anything to say to you in the service He will say it.

PROBLEMS

We need to stop thinking about everything in terms of problems and to begin living as though life was an adventure. We are so enslaved by the idea of security we are afraid to launch out and live. We want someone to solve our problems. Problems were not meant to be solved. They were meant to be lived. Faith in God will send you forth with courage to live and with joy in the battle. The very problem you face can be your call to adventure.

CHARITY

The only way we can live together in harmony is in Christian charity. Living in charity with others means we major in their goodness rather than their badness, their virtue rather than their vice. It means seeking to live with others in kindness and in courtesy without pushing ourselves up by pushing them down. Jesus said, "Whatsoever ye would that men should do to you, do ye even to them."

CONFORMITY

Today, more than ever before, is an age of conformity. The propaganda from business and labor and government tends to see that we think as we should think, buy as we should buy, love as we should love and hate as we should hate.

Unfortunately the church has been caught in this wave of conformity. It witnesses in a way not to offend anybody, in a way not to be thought of as peculiar. The church has been watered down. But we are still the "called" of God and we must say loudly with our lives, as well as with words, "that no man cometh unto the Father but by Him." And maybe once more we will be found worthy of the gift of the Holy Spirit of God. This gift by which the world may again be turned upside down.

PREACHERS

It is right interesting to be a clergyman today. It requires, among other qualities, a sense of humor lest you take yourself more seriously than other people take you. Many people feel that since the preacher is against sin they don't have to be. With all this is the high privilege of walking with people in their deep valleys.

ACKNOWLEDGEMENTS

North Avenue Presbyterian Church, the publisher of TOUCH OF THE SHEPHERD: Reflections on the Life of Vernon S. Broyles, Jr., is most grateful and appreciative to the following people who helped to make the publication of this book possible:

To Celestine Sibley, for without her long and enduring friendship with Dr. Broyles this tribute could not have been written. Celestine has managed to capture the essence of the life of Dr. Broyles, his impact on friends and associates, and his contributions to the city of Atlanta.

To Dr. Broyles's widow, Eloise Darby Broyles, and the children, Bena Broyles Cates, Vernon S. Broyles, III, and Betsy Broyles Moore, all of whom provided insights into life in the Broyles family.

And to those associates of Dr. Broyles who played a part in bringing this extraordinary life story from idea to published book: Dr. James E. Long, Senior Pastor of North

AvenuePresbyterian Church; Dr. D. Wayne Smith, Associate Chaplain, Big Canoe Chapel; and Dr. William W. Pressly, first Headmaster of Westminster Schools, each of whom contributed outstanding support to this project.

Special thanks is due to the many people who submitted the photographs used in the book. We regret that, because of the lack of space, we can not name each of you, but, nonetheless, your contributions are greatly appreciated.

We are especially indebted to Donna Fullilove for her archival research, and to Victoria MacKay for the photographs of Dr. Broyles's days as board chair for Westminster Schools, and to Elizabeth Flinn, Charlene Terrell, Glad Eldridge, and Kathleen Ingram for providing additional photographs for the book.

The back cover photograph of Dr. Broyles was taken by Gittings Studio of Atlanta, and is used with the permission of Mrs. Eloise Broyles.

This book contains many stories of individuals and families who found great strength and love in their relationship with Dr. Broyles. For each story told, there are dozens more untold. Dr. Broyles's death cut short the inter-views with Celestine Sibley, but no amount of time would have been sufficient to tell the whole story of what Vernon Broyles meant to the thousands who passed his way.

We would not be complete in our expression of appreciation without thanking everyone who contributed to this project, turning an idea into a finished book.

The Broyles Memorial
Planning Committee